TURN UP THE WICK!

BY FRANK BEAMER
WITH CHRIS COLSTON

An **EPIC SPORTS** Book

Front cover and back cover photos by Steve Helber, AP/Wide World.

Cover Design by: Chris Kozlowski, Dallas, Tex.
Book Design by: Lori Leath-Smith of Lori Smith Design, Birmingham, Ala.
Published by: Epic Sports, Birmingham, Ala.

INTRODUCTION

EVERYBODY HAS their quirks, and I certainly have mine. There are some things I just hate to do, and putting gas in the car is one of them. It has nothing to do with my childhood accident. I just hate doing it.

I remember one of my first dates with my wife, Cheryl. This was right after I had graduated from college, and I was recovering from appendicitis. I was living in Radford, where I would soon begin coaching as an assistant at Radford High.

Cheryl lived in Richmond, and was driving down with some friends. So I was going to meet her at the service station out by Interstate 81, in Christiansburg.

I guess I waited at that service station for about 20 minutes.

Finally Cheryl arrived, and we got in my car and set out toward Radford on I-81. After traveling about two miles I ran out of gas.

You can imagine she was a little upset, especially after I had just been at the gas station. So after she stopped fussing at me we had to start walking back to the gas station. Once there, we borrowed a five-gallon tank full of gas and Cheryl had to carry it, because of my appendicitis.

Needless to say, we survived that ordeal — and since then I've tried to pay more attention to how much gas is in the tank.

Cheryl hung in there with me that day and she's still there — always believing in me, always in my corner.

There have also been so many other good people who have been there through the years: My son, Shane, a senior on the Tech varsity who snapped on punts during this special season; my daughter, Casey, who as a freshman enjoyed the many thrills of Tech's unbelievably loud student section; my parents, Raymond and Herma; my brother, Barnett; my sisters, Billie Jean and Betty; Cheryl's parents, Mike and Lindy Oakley; my coaches, Tommy Thompson and Jerry Claiborne; the coaches who hired me, Harold Absher, Norm Lineburg; Bobby Ross, Art Baker and Mike Gottfried; Dutch Baughman, who hired me at Tech; the university presidents I've worked for, all those great assistant coaches who did all the really hard work, and the players at Radford High, Maryland, The Citadel, Murray State and Virginia Tech who made all of this so special.

It's been an unforgettable run so far. I can't wait to see what lies ahead.

— F.B.

EDITOR'S NOTE

L A S T   F A L L , Virginia Tech's incredible journey to New Orleans and the National Championship Game against Florida State in the Sugar Bowl grabbed the curiosity of America.

From coast to coast, fans who had never heard of a Hokie before were amazed by the passing and running of freshman quarterback Michael Vick, Shyrone Stith's bulldozing romps and a stingy defense that was probably the best in college football in 1999.

By mid-November, Virginia Tech baseball hats, t-shirts and sweatshirts could be seen in malls, in restaurants and airports everywhere you traveled.

I was fortunate to chronicle Tech's 1999 season in the commemorative book, *Hokie High*, which was published in January 2000 in conjunction with The Roanoke Times.

It was in this effort that I was able to fully appreciate and understand the special qualities of the man who led the Hokies, Frank Beamer.

He is a lot like Bear Bryant, whom I worked for as a student at the University of Alabama in the late 1970's. Beamer is country smart, emotionally-charged, dedicated and driven to build his alma mater into one of college football's top Mecca's.

It is a similar feat that Knute Rockne achieved at Notre

Dame in the 1920's, Jock Sutherland did at Pitt in the 1930's, Red Blaik demonstrated at West Point in the 1940's, Bud Wilkinson performed at Oklahoma in the 1950's, and Bear Bryant orchestrated at Alabama in the 1960's and 70's.

Beamer fits in this special group.

He has led Virginia Tech to its greatest hour on the gridiron — and the best is yet to come.

As we were preparing this book and discussing possible titles, I kept hearing stories of a unique phrase often used by the coach when the game, or a practice, got intense. The phrase was "Turn Up the Wick!"

Undoubtedly, it best describes Beamer's will to win — whether it be in football, on the golf course or during his daily racquetball games.

— Mike Bynum
May 10, 2000

CONTENTS

1

A NIGHT TO REMEMBER

I LOOK BACK on it now and it all seems like a blur.

Backup tailback Andre Kendrick had just scored on a six-yard run late in the third quarter of the 2000 National Championship game in the Sugar Bowl. Trailing Florida State, 28-7, and on the verge of being blown out, we had roared back. Now, with 2:13 left in the third quarter, we led, 29-28, and our fans were rocking the New Orleans Superdome.

To appreciate what our fans felt, you have to understand that just seven years earlier, we won only two games. My record after six years was an unimpressive 24-40-2. Most coaches don't survive that. Maybe I shouldn't have survived that. But there was a mutual faith at Virginia Tech, and we didn't dwell on what we could not control. We just tried to get better.

And now, on Tuesday, Jan. 4, 2000, we were on the verge of

beating Florida State for the National Championship in the Sugar Bowl.

I felt a surge of excitement, because I knew exactly what was at stake here. I felt all along — and I still do — that if we played our normal game, we would have beaten Florida State. We normally get points out of our kicking game and this time we gave them up. And we normally don't give up long plays. Then all of a sudden we've got a couple of them in this ballgame and that meant our downfall.

We had a punt blocked for a touchdown. The great Peter Warrick returned a punt 59 yards for another score. We failed on a fake field goal and a fake punt.

That was too much to overcome and the Seminoles beat us, 46-29, giving head coach Bobby Bowden his first undefeated season.

After we had taken that third-quarter lead, I felt a tingling in my stomach. I was excited, but I was also worried. We hadn't gotten more points out of our opportunities, and in football that usually comes back to haunt you. And although we had owned the third quarter, we only led by one. That's nothing when you're playing Florida State, a team that can score on you quickly. So even when we took that lead, I was thinking, "we should be ahead by more than this."

To this day, I still haven't looked at the videotape of that game. You never know how many opportunities you're going to have to win a national championship. I didn't think about this in the third quarter, but afterward, I was so happy that we made that comeback. I mean, it would have been a miserable thing if we had gotten beat, 57-7. Some members of the media thought we didn't deserve to be playing for the national championship because of our perceived weak schedule, and then they could point to the score and say, "see?" Instead it turned out to be one of the better championship games that has been played.

Although we trailed, 28-14, at halftime, I told the kids, "We've got them right where we want them." I know that sounds a little crazy, but that's what I said. We knew we could play with Florida State. We had done some things that were not typical of our football team, and yet we had closed the game before the half and had some momentum. We were in position.

I told our guys, "All we have to do is go be ourselves." And, in the third quarter, that's kind of what happened. Of course, it helps to have a quarterback like Michael Vick when you're trying to change things around.

It's funny. Every time the Seminoles scored, it came on big plays. It's not like they were ripping off 10 to 15 yards a pop. That's when you start worrying. They had that blocked kick at our 10-yard line where one of their interior guys kind of grabbed one of our guys. He got him turned around and All-ACC linebacker Tommy Polley got through to block the kick. Jeff Chaney recovered the ball at the six and ran it in for the score.

On that Warrick punt return, we got a short kick and then we didn't cover like we normally do, and Warrick being so quick, he was coming back at us so fast, then all of sudden it was a touchdown. It wasn't a normal Jimmy Kibble punt and Warrick wasn't your normal kick returner, and our punt coverage guys didn't keep their lanes very well. Everything got out of sequence, and that was not like us at all.

And then FSU got that 63-yard pass from quarterback Chris Weinke to receiver Ron Dugans. That hurt. Our defender was on top of the play, but he picked an angle over the top and just barely missed the ball. Dugans caught it and there he went. As much as you dislike long plays, and as much as you realize that you can't allow long plays if you want to stay in the ballgame, well, it's a lot better to have it that way than to be getting hit with 10 yards here, 12 there, 15 there, relentless, wearing you down play after play. It was just those four or five plays.

I don't know if the pressure got to me or what, but at half-time, I said, "We've got them right where we want them." The Seminoles were cocky, confident. I said all we have to do is just get those four or five plays in the second half and be ourselves and, believe me, we'll win this thing.

We were familiar with Florida State. We played them in 1988, 1989, 1990 and 1991 and came darn close to beating them in 1990, at Tallahassee.

I remember the first time we played them. It was 1988, and FSU was ranked No. 5 and had Deion Sanders. It was our first trip to Tallahassee, and we had heard stories about their mascot — Chief Osceola — and how he rode out on the field on his Appaloosa horse and stuck a flaming spear into the ground at midfield before the game.

Well, we had an emotional linebacker, Don Stokes, who was really fired up. I mean he really got worked up into a frenzy, and after warmups he came into the locker room and started cursing and punching lockers and saying he was going to tackle that damn Appaloosa horse. He kept going on about it and pretty soon we got the idea that he was actually going to go out there and tackle that damn Appaloosa horse.

I didn't quite know what to do. I knew our team needed to be fired up to go out there and play these guys, so I didn't want to calm down Don too much. But we couldn't have him going out there and trying to tackle their horse. So finally I pulled aside assistant coach Billy Hite.

"Billy," I said. "How about taking care of Don for me."

Billy kinda nodded his head. Then about a minute later he returned.

"Coach," he said, "what exactly were you, uh, wanting me to do?"

I wasn't sure, but I knew we had to do something. We got out on the field and I put on my headset. I'm watching Don pretty close.

"Billy, Billy," I said into my headset. "Don's edging out onto the field toward that horse."

I kept watching.

"Billy, he's getting closer, Billy," I said.

Finally, Billy clicked on the microphone to his headset.

"Coach," he said, "if Don wants to tackle that damn horse, there's not a whole lot I'm gonna be able to do about it."

Billy ended up kind of trailing Don out there on the field, but Don never did tackle that horse. I don't know, maybe he got up close and realized how big the thing was.

I'll tell you what. I'll never forget that 1990 game at Tallahassee. It was late September and FSU was ranked No. 2 in the nation. We led, 21-3, midway through the second quarter. They made a run but we still led, 28-25, late in the game with the ball at our 38-yard line after a Roger Garland interception.

Their cornerback Terrell Buckley intercepted Will Furrer's pass and he made this high-stepping dazzling 53-yard return for a score. Now we're trailing, 32-28, with four minutes to go, but we're driving for the winning touchdown. We've got the momentum and they're having a hard time stopping us.

On third-and-two at the FSU 33, our great little tailback, Vaughn Hebron, had made the first down and was trying for extra yardage. Their linebacker, Kirk Carruthers, came over and chopped across Vaughn's arms and knocked the ball loose. The ball hit the ground, took one bounce and went right into the arms of defensive back Errol McCorvey on the dead run. He sprinted 77 yards for a touchdown.

It was a freaky play, and FSU won, 39-28. After the game, Bobby Bowden came out to midfield to shake hands and he said, in that famous drawl of his, "Frank, wasn't that just the BEST game?"

I thought to myself, "It might have been good for you, but man, my stomach hurts." I got the idea he never felt like he was in danger of losing that game. But it about killed me.

13

So when we took that lead in the third quarter of the Sugar Bowl, I can tell you exactly what I was thinking. I was thinking, "man, I want to win this game, and after it's over, go up to Bowden and shake his hand."

And then, with all due respect, I'd say with a smile, "Bobby, wasn't that just the BEST game?"

That would have been fun, but it wasn't to be. The big play of the game came early in the fourth quarter when Florida State went for it on fourth-and-one from their own 46. I'm not sure they felt like they could stop Michael Vick. If we had stopped them on that fourth-down play, I think the game had a chance to really turn our way because now we've got field position, we just stopped them and we are inside their 50. In any game you can go back and look at four or five plays and say that.

Anyway, it was a heck of an experience, a heck of a night out of my life. And I want to get back there and get it right.

But no, I still haven't gone back and looked at the tape of that game. When you have a chance to win a national championship and you don't do it, that's something that stays with you awhile. But I think one day I will watch the tape.

One day when I want to feel some pain again.

You talk about pain. There was pain in that locker room after that one. We have a tradition that we've had the last couple of years, after the last game of the season. We let each one of our seniors express themselves. It's always a tough time, because you're saying goodbye. Those are guys who are never going to be in a locker room with you again.

And there were some really special people in that locker room. The 1999 Big East Defensive Player of the Year, Corey Moore. What a great, great leader. Defensive end John Engelberger. What a guy. He says he doesn't like to talk to the press, but he gets quoted more than anybody I've ever seen. John's a really smart guy and he kind of sees through people. In his own way, John was a very important leader to Virginia Tech and that football team.

Then we had some guys like wide receiver Ricky Hall, whose mother was sick before the game and then passed away. And he really wanted to play but had that broken foot.

Defensive tackle Nathaniel Williams played his last game, and there were times we thought his career might be over long before the Sugar Bowl. He overcame alcoholism. He's really a different guy right now. Let me give you an example of how he matured during his senior year. Every year, to start spring drills, we have a 6 a.m. workout. It's kind of a toughness thing. Sets the tone for the season. Well, the day before we started our 2000 spring practice he came into our reception area outside John Ballein's office. John is the assistant athletic director for football operations.

"I wish I was getting up for that 6 a.m. drill," he told our secretary, Kristie Verniel.

Last year at this time, he was moaning groaning about getting up so early. But now he was saying how he would love another year to play college football.

There were so many great seniors in that locker room. Placekicker Shayne Graham, who kicked the field goal against West Virginia to keep our winning streak alive. Linebacker Jamel Smith, defensive tackle Carl Bradley, defensive end Chris Cyrus, punter Jimmy Kibble, cornerback Anthony Midget, centers Tim Schnecker and Keith Short. Deep snapper Cliff Anders. Holder Caleb Hurd. Steven Hunt. Daniel Nihipali. Greg Shockley. My son, Shane.

Linebacker Michael Hawkes. He was the heart of the team, really. A guy who was kinda the glue. He wasn't the most talented, but he was as hardworking as anyone we've had here. Everyone around him realized how much he put into this football team. He's not a big talker, but I'm telling you, all these guys would rally behind him because he had such a great work ethic.

Then there were a couple of underclassmen. We didn't know for sure then, but they had played their last game at Tech: cornerback Ike Charlton and running back Shyrone Stith.

We were all in there crying. It was a real "together" moment. And the governor of Virginia, Jim Gilmore, was waiting outside. John Ballein knew me well enough not to interrupt in a time like that. Those players come first and nothing was going to interrupt it. After we were finished with the seniors I started to walk away, and that's when John told me the President of the United States was on the phone.

John said I gave him a look he will never forget.

I'm thinking, "the President? He wouldn't call here. He only calls the winning team." I thought someone was pulling my leg. But John led me to this phone in the training room, and I guess I passed the Governor on the way. I picked up the phone.

It was President Clinton.

"I really enjoyed the heart your football team showed," he said. He complimented our effort some more, then he said, "This wasn't the first time I have seen you play this year. I really enjoy your style."

I'll be honest with you. I didn't think he quite sounded the way he sounds on television. Halfway through the conversation, the thought that's running through my mind is, "Is this REALLY the President?"

Then I returned to the dressing room, where Governor Gilmore said a couple of words to the team. That was all great, but you have to understand something. In dressing rooms, you have some of your greatest moments in sports. You've been in there crying both ways. You're crying because you got beat, crying because you won and then you put the final game into that, oh man. There is a real happiness, yet there is a real sadness, too.

That mood overrides everything.

Don't get me wrong. I was very appreciative that the President of the United States took the time to call the losing locker room. That says a lot. But I think there is only so much emotion you can absorb in one night. And the prevailing thing here was a group of players who played hard, we didn't meet our goal and now these guys aren't going to be back in uniform again and my son, Shane, is one of them. And then the governor was there, and I appreciated that, too. But the overriding emotion, for me, wasn't talking to the President.

It was being with those special seniors one last time.

2

WHEN LIFE TURNED IN A DIFFERENT DIRECTION

I WAS BORN October 18, 1946, in Mt. Airy, North Carolina, which was the nearest hospital to Fancy Gap, Virginia. If you have never heard of Fancy Gap, well, let's just say it's a suburb of Hillsville, located in the mountains of Southwest Virginia. If you've never heard of Hillsville, that tells you something about the size of Fancy Gap.

I was the youngest of four children.

My brother, Barnett (pronounced BARN it) is five years older than me. My sisters, Billie Jean and Betty, are seven and two years older.

My parents, Raymond and Herma, had a 70-acre farm, but we really didn't farm. We had a garden and some cows and I cut and baled hay in the summer, but we didn't actually raise crops.

I had a good childhood. But my life took a turn one afternoon in 1954, when I was seven years old.

It was early June and school had just let out for the summer. It was around lunchtime. Dad was at work, and mom and my sisters were at my grandmother's house. At the house we had an open double garage, and a bunch of papers and leaves had blown in there, so dad had asked us to clean it out that day. We had done some painting earlier, and had used a gallon jug of gasoline to clean the brushes, and the jug was sitting there in the garage, with a little bit of gasoline still in it.

We built a fire outside, near a little creek along the garage. We burned garbage there all the time.

Barnett and I carried some trash out to the fire and pushed it around with our brooms. I went back into the garage with the broom to get some more trash.

What happened next is still a blur. I guess the jug tipped over and rolled toward me. I might have kicked it away and some of the gasoline sloshed up. There must have been some ashes smoldering in the broom.

I remember an explosion. It hit me right in the face. It happened so fast.

I screamed and ran outside. Barnett was in the garage and he rushed over and caught me and rolled me over on the grass, trying to put out the fire. He threw dirt on me and got it out.

I ran inside and filled the bathtub with water and sat down. Mom came home, saw me and took me to the doctor, but I don't think anybody realized how badly I was burned. I had burns on the right side of my face, my neck, my right arm and my shoulders, and that night everything started blistering. I remember laying awake in bed in the dark all night. It just hurt so bad.

The next day they took me to the hospital, and I stayed there through most of the fall.

For the next four years I underwent something like 30

operations of varying degrees. They couldn't get skin to grow under my chin, because there was so much movement there. They grafted skin from my stomach, they grafted skin from my thighs, but they couldn't fix it. The skin wouldn't take. We had all of these unsuccessful operations, and they did them in the summer, and then when it was the fall they would wait again till the next summer. It wasn't something, as a child, I looked forward to.

This one doctor, Dr. James Martin, did something that really kind of blew my mind back then. It was probably ahead of its time. He took some of my skin and fed it in through a tube hooked to the top and bottom of my back. It was just a tube of skin and then they got it growing and it was the strangest thing, I have to tell you. So when it got growing healthy, they took a piece at the bottom and brought it around to my face. He got it going for a couple of weeks.

Then he took a piece of skin from the top of my back and brought the rest of it around and that's how the skin got healed on my neck.

It wasn't like there was a lot of discussion about all of this. Mom was like, "This is what has to happen, and let's go." But one time they put me to sleep for one of the operations, and I guess I got so used to the medication that I didn't wake up for about a day and a half or so.

It put quite a scare into everybody. For the next two operations they didn't put me to sleep. They just numbed me. They were working on putting this tube together on my back, and I felt them cutting my skin.

It was the longest two hours I've ever spent in my life.

Dr. Martin used those operations to try to get more of the puffiness out of my face. There were two more operations scheduled to get the rest of it out.

And then Dr. Martin died of a heart attack.

I had a chance to see another doctor, who would try a

couple more operations to get the puffiness out, but at that time I said I had enough. I let it go, and that's why my neck is probably a little puffy. Because Dr. Martin never had a chance to finish up his work.

There were times I've thought of seeing a plastic surgeon to take the puffiness out and make my face smoother. But now I never think about it very much. I remember what my mom said. "It's what you have, and that's it." It's just been there, and as much as I wish it wasn't there, it's there. So I get on with it. It's part of who I am. And my wife, Cheryl, has always been great. It's never been a big issue with her.

It was the type of deal where this was what was going to happen and this was what I was going to do. Part of that was me, and part of that was Barnett, and part of that was the love of my parents.

Dad worked for the Virginia Highway Department as an Assistant Highway Engineer. Mom was a teacher. I went to a one-room schoolhouse my first four years. Then they built a new elementary school for grades one through seven and my mom was my fifth-grade teacher. I remember it because she absolutely was tougher on me than anyone else in that class. If she was out of the room and came back and there was talking going on, she would paddle me first.

I think I got a lot of my leadership qualities from her. Coming in, taking control of a situation, being in charge, I got all of that from her. Even now, at family events, you know she's going to be in charge. But she's also very caring. She always is concerned that everybody is happy, that everything is running well. She just went through heart bypass surgery a couple of years ago, but she's working out, staying in shape. She's 84 years old and still comes to every ballgame. She has a toughness about her. When I was going through my burn surgeries, she was the one who was most involved. She would drive me to the hospital in Pulaski, an hour or so each way, four or five times a week. I mean there is just a real toughness about her.

When I was first burned and I was lying there in the hospital, feeling very sorry for myself, she made me get up and walk down the hall. We walked past three or four doors before finding someone who was in a lot worse shape than me.

"We have problems," she said. "But we don't have nearly as many problems as some of these people, so just be thankful for what's taking place and then let's get on with getting well."

She wanted to know what other operations I needed to have. Her deal was, "Let's have them and let's get it done." All those times we rode to Pulaski, I can never remember her feeling sorry for us. I can never remember her ever saying something like "boy, I wish we could ..." or complaining about doing that. She never did that.

Although my dad was a low-key guy, you always knew when he meant business, because his mood changed a little bit. But he didn't change very often, and then he just kind of rode with the punches and I think I'm a little bit like that. He had his chances to move, but he was very content living in Carroll County. I think there was a time when I was in the seventh grade where he could have taken a promotion and we would have moved. It was a pretty dramatic time but he decided not to take it.

But although he stayed in an ordinary situation, he would venture out and do something out of the ordinary. I can remember him taking this Dale Carnegie course in public speaking. So here was a guy from Fancy Gap out talking to this group at a particular function. He was a guy who kinda fit into any kind of situation, but he was always true to himself. I always admired that. Maybe I got some of that from him.

Sports was a way of life for me growing up, but it wasn't easy. It wasn't like we had these buses taking us home after football practice. It wasn't like you knew you'd finish practice at 6 p.m. and be home by 6:30. It just wasn't like that. So, you had to really want to do it.

I lived seven miles from the high school, so I had to hitch-hike home. Hillsville High School was at the other end of Route 52, which went right through Fancy Gap and on to Mt. Airy. The high school was at the other end of Hillsville. Now don't get me wrong, Hillsville is not a big city, but I'd have to walk a mile, maybe two, through town, until I found someone to pick me up.

At that time, Interstate 77 wasn't built, so there was a lot of traffic on 52, with a lot of strangers driving through. There were always two or three of us, and we always hoped a next door neighbor would be coming through there pretty soon to pick us up. Most of the time that was the case, but I can remember times being in a car with somebody I didn't know and hoping that they would let me out.

I always had a supportive family. There were no questions; you were going to play sports. In my family, that was the thing to do. Any kind of competition on TV, my dad would watch it. He'd sit there and watch a hockey game, and he didn't know one rule of hockey. He never played golf, but he'd sit and watch golf on a Sunday afternoon. He loved baseball and was a big New York Giants fan. When they moved to San Francisco, he'd be up at 4 a.m. trying to get the West Coast scores.

Growing up on that farm was great motivation. I think if I remember anything, it was probably working in those hay fields. How hot they were, and you had to wear long sleeve shirts or your arms would get all scratched up from the hay. I probably never did take to farm work as seriously as dad would have liked.

I remember one time I had to help one of our neighbors, Mr. Canady Marshall, bale some hay. He was an older gentle-man who always kept a jug of ice water for drinking. It was always so cold nobody could drink it but him. It was a hot day and we broke for lunch. I just relaxed in the pickup truck with my sandwich, and I took a little nap.

Break time was soon over and instead of waking me; Mr. Marshall took a little of that ice water and dribbled it down my face. I bolted up; wild-eyed, ready to whip somebody I was so mad. The old man told Barnett, "I'll never do that again. I thought that boy was going to attack me."

When I was lifting those bales of hay, and fighting with my sisters over who had to milk that extra cow or who had to wash the milk strainer, I knew there had to be a better way to live. That's nothing against farmers, but I wanted to do something different.

Don't get me wrong. We had a good house to live in. We were comfortable. The house I grew up in is still there. Mom rents it out. I haven't been there in a long time. I know it didn't have a shower, just a bathtub. I think that's why I like taking showers so much today.

There was a little hill of dirt leading into that garage behind the house, and it made a perfect pitching mound. I drew a square on the far wall of the garage, and it was a strike if you could hit that square. We also put a basketball goal in there. But the problem was the rafters, so there were only certain places where you had a clear shot at the basket. So if you knew those spots, you had a distinct home-court advantage.

The front yard of the house wasn't real big, but I guess it was big enough. That's where I grew up playing football with Barnett and his friends. They were all about five years older than me, and at that age, that's a huge difference. Barnett always picked me to be on his team, but he expected me to play as well as everybody else. Everybody else was so much bigger than me, so I had to be tough.

When there were just the two of us there, Barnett and I used to play this game where one of us would center the ball to the other guy, who would try to run past him to score. I know he would hit me pretty good. A couple of times he'd run over me and push my face into the ground and I would cry.

"You can't cry," he said. "You've got to be tough."

Barnett would get me to play catch with him. He'd throw me fastballs, curveballs, everything, as hard as he could, and he expected me to catch them all. Sometimes I did, and sometimes it would bounce and hit me in the face. He always pushed me to succeed.

It was a tough time, recovering from the burns. But there was only one way to go. I had to take care of it and go on. At the time, there was concern about my face, of course, but also my arm. My right arm, my throwing arm, was badly burned, so part of this whole thing was getting back the use of that arm. And if you're an athlete, you've got to be able to throw.

So Barnett used to get me out there throwing the football with him. It was not a big deal; it was just that kind of thing where we were going to do this to get my arm ready to play. I never had a choice about it.

We never really talked about the accident. We just put the thing behind us. We could talk about "what-if," but there was no point in it. There was no sense in wasting time dwelling on it. But during his senior year, he wrote a theme paper on his greatest thrill.

He said it was seeing me throw a football again after my accident.

Growing up, everybody just treated me like anybody else. I can never remember getting teased about my scars. I never had many confrontations with people.

But I do remember one. It didn't have anything to do with my scars.

I was in the ninth or 10th grade. There was a guy from the other end of the county from where I was from and he didn't play any sports. I don't know if that was it or not, but he kept bumping into me in the hallway. I didn't know what was going on.

One day we were out behind the school. We didn't have a gym, but we had some basketball courts and goals with these chain link nets behind the school. I loved to play basketball, and after lunch we'd go back there and play until the next period. Well, one day he told me he was going to meet me out at the basketball court and I thought, aw, geez.

So, I ate my lunch, and I was just nervous as heck. I didn't know if I could take him or if he'd take me, but I knew it was going to be like the fight at the OK Corral. So, we went out there after lunch and we were playing ball and all of a sudden I saw him walk around the corner of the building. He walked right up and he's had two or three of his buddies behind him. But I wasn't going to back down because there were a bunch of guys out there. You know how that is.

This guy walked up to me, and the only thing I knew was that I wasn't going to be asking any questions. I just started flailing. It seemed like it went on for about five minutes, although it couldn't have been more than 30 seconds. Thank goodness they pulled us apart because I had used myself up. But I guess you could say I got the better of him.

To this day, I don't know why he wanted to fight me. The only thing I can figure was that I played sports, and he didn't.

3

FROM HILLSVILLE
TO HOKIELAND

HILLSVILLE ISN'T a hotbed of high school talent. It's a small place. Back in the 1960's, our idea of fun was a dance after the game in the high school cafeteria. Then we'd take a couple of swings around the local hangout, Corney's Drive-In, where the servers came out to your car to take your order. That place had great hot dogs. That's where everybody would gather.

If you wanted to see someone over in Galax, then you'd go to the bowling alley. The other big thing then was the VFW dances.

I was my senior class president, and we planned a senior trip to New York City. To raise money for the trip we held dances every two weeks at the VFW. And we delivered Krispy Kreme doughnuts every Saturday morning, door to door. It took awhile, but we raised enough money for the trip.

During that trip to New York, we took a side trip to Atlantic City. Some of the kids had gotten hold of some beer. I'm not going to mention this guy's name because he's a prominent lawyer now, but he drank a little too much.

Anyway, he was getting ornery and wanted to hit the town. I tried to calm him down and tell him that was not something he needed to do. He kept going on about going out, so I just hit him. Knocked him clean out. Now, with the way he was feeling, it didn't take much. He was out cold.

And to this day he still hasn't forgiven me. He doesn't understand why I clocked him, but I was just trying to keep him out of trouble.

Even though I was on the football team, I was also a member of the Hillsville High School Band. I played trombone. The band director James Calabrese, a real dynamic guy, had arrived in Hillsville and really generated a lot of enthusiasm for the band. My freshman year I was on the jayvee band team, and the varsity was scheduled to play at the Apple Blossom Festival in Winchester, Va.

This was a big deal because they were going on these nice new Greyhound buses. I really wanted to go, and the varsity needed one more person to carry a tuba in the back row.

It was just for show; the person didn't have to actually play the tuba. They just needed to even out the row. So they scheduled a "march-off" between four of us. We would march with the tuba and Mr. Calabrese would choose a winner.

I got nervous as heck about it, which was hard to understand because all I had to do was march with a tuba. I was an athlete, so I could march, now.

But I lost. I was heartbroken over it. Three days later, Mr. Calabrese came to me.

"We still need one more person to go on this trip," he said.

"What for?" I asked.

"We need two people to walk in front of the band with our banner," he said, "and we only have one person."

"I'll do it!" I said.

"There's just one catch," Mr. Calabrese said.

"What's that?"

"We only have one uniform left. You have to be able to fit into the uniform or you can't go."

That uniform was a little tight, I admit. But I squeezed into it and led the band in the Cherry Blossom Festival.

Going from the back row to the front row like that, I guess I've been lucky all my life.

LIFE IN HILLSVILLE was actually pretty neat. If we wanted to see a movie, we had several choices. We had a tiny little theatre in Hillsville, where it was about five steps from the front door to the seating area. I mean, you walked in, and there was the concession stand, and boom, you're inside the theatre. Cheryl thought that was so funny. And there were drive-in theatres in Galax and Mount Airy, so there were plenty of places to watch movies.

I can never remember lifting a single weight in high school. We'd just go from one sport to the other to keep in shape. Even in the summer, after baseball, I can't remember any special football training or weightlifting.

Even when I was at Tech, we didn't lift weights the way it's done now. We had a room upstairs in Cassell Coliseum and everything we did was quick-oriented. You'd see how many times you could press a barbell, but there wasn't nearly the emphasis that there is today. In the offseason we'd get on mats and wrestle. That was a big toughness deal. Everybody would throw each other around and see who would come out of it. It was tough. We lost some guys off the team that way.

I liked basketball, but I was just an average player. I could shoot a little and get in there and scrap around.

In baseball, I played center fielder and batted leadoff. I also pitched a little but I was never any good at it. That was something I never quite understood, because I could really throw a football. But I couldn't pitch a baseball.

Football was always my game. I could always figure it out. The game always made sense to me. I see players now who just sort of run around out there and the game doesn't seem to make sense to them. But I never would have made it to Tech if it wasn't for my high school coach, Tommy Thompson.

And I don't think I would have received a scholarship to Tech unless I had thrown a lot of touchdown passes in high school. And it was because of Coach Thompson's offense.

He was a really neat guy. An amazing guy. He just loved studying football and being around coaches, picking their brains, trying to learn as much as he could. In the offseason he had spent a week in Baltimore with the Colts and Johnny Unitas, learning their passing offense. And he comes back to Hillsville High School with the Baltimore Colts' passing game.

This is the early 1960's, so this was kind of unusual. But that's the kind of guy he was. All of sudden we're passing the ball all over the place in high school and I ended up throwing like 43 touchdown passes in two years. If I hadn't done that, I don't know if I'd have gotten a scholarship to Virginia Tech. And I'm pretty sure I never would have gotten the head coaching job at Tech unless I had been an alumnus, so I really owe everything to Coach Thompson. He made a real difference in my life.

After we upset ninth-ranked West Virginia in 1989, he came into my office on Monday morning with a plaque that had the date of the game engraved on it. He realized how important that win was for Tech, and for me. Then, later that week, he had a heart attack and died. He's one of the people I wish was around to see our success today.

My senior year we were playing Blacksburg High School for the district championship. Coach Thompson went to the shot-gun formation because he was concerned about protection. So all I did was throw the ball and then run a sweep one way or the other, and a couple of off-tackle plays. Well, I was off running a sweep and this guy, Gary McCoy — he's the principal at Blacksburg Middle School now — hit me. I never saw him. He's a short, stocky guy and he clipped my feet right out from under me.

I went flying up in the air and came down on my head.

I got up real slow. I was woozy. I needed to come out so I began waving my hand at Coach Thompson.

But he thought I was saying, "I'm OK!"

I kept waiting for somebody to come in for me and nobody came in. I was still dazed, but I knew enough to call a running play. I handed off the ball and then my head cleared and I was OK after that. Virginia Tech head football coach Jerry Claiborne was at the game, and when it was over he came up to Coach Thompson.

"Any kid who can land on his head and demand to stay in the game deserves a scholarship to Virginia Tech," he said.

Neither one ever realized I was actually begging to come out of the game.

We ended up losing that one. Even now I have a hard time sleeping after a loss, but it was worse then. Barnett and I shared a room with bunk beds and I slept on the top bunk. In the middle of the night I had nightmares about the game and tumbled onto the floor. When I came to, I was up against a chair shoved against the closet. Barnett had a scared look on his face.

"What happened?" I said.

"I don't know," Barnett said, his eyes wide. "I heard you screaming, 'Get 'em! Get 'em! Get 'em!' You pushed all the furniture up against the wall like you were trying to tackle it. Then you started yelling, 'You're not going to score! You're not going to score!' "

I had all kinds of problems with my head that year. During the middle of basketball season I was driving home on a Sunday afternoon and approached a hill. There was a service station there, and I saw some neighbors from school. I turned to wave, and as I came over the hill I saw a car stopped, waiting to make a left turn. This was a two-lane road so there was nowhere to go. I swerved but hit it from behind. I got thrown forward and banged my head against the windshield. There was blood all over the place. Barnett had to come to get me afterward.

I knew I was bleeding badly, but my head kind of went numb. I couldn't feel any pain.

"How does it look?" I asked him on the way to the hospital.

"It looks serious," he said.

They were picking glass out of my head for what seemed like weeks. I took about 40-50 stitches and had my head wrapped up in bandages. Time passed and it was near the end of basketball season, and I wanted to play. We weren't very good, and we played all of our "home" games at the Hillsville VFW, then later at the Galax YMCA after the VFW burned. Nobody could understand why I wanted to come back and risk getting hit on the head.

But I just didn't want to quit like that.

So I went out there with my head covered in a white bandage and played in that last game. I guess it was just my competitive nature coming through.

To top it all off, that spring I was playing center field for the baseball team. There was a routine fly ball and I settled under it. I took my eye off the ball for a second to check the runner, and WHAM, that ball hit me right on the forehead.

My dad and a friend of his, Johnny Howlett, were watching from the stands.

"I think Frankie needs to grow some grass on his head,"

Johnny told dad. "If he don't get some padding up there, he's going to get killed."

THAT SPRING, I got letters from William and Mary and Richmond and VMI. Wake Forest was somewhat interested. So was Tulane. I had made some All-Southeastern Region all-star teams, and you could tell Tulane was recruiting off that list, because they ended up inviting most of the all-stars down there for a weekend visit. Fortunately, I was one of those invited on the trip.

It was the first time I had ever been on a plane. I was scared to death.

Someone asked me if I was going to visit Bourbon Street, and I didn't know what they were talking about.

The thing about that trip I remember most was walking into head coach Tommy O'Boyle's office. You should have seen the look on his face. Here's this hot quarterback prospect he's brought in all the way from Virginia, and I walk in and you know I'm only about 5-foot-9. I could just tell he was expecting something else. You could just see him thinking, "boy, did we screw this thing up."

I ended up spending most of my recruiting trip in the piano bar at this place called Pat O'Brien's, which is famous for a drink called a "Hurricane." Once I got back to Blacksburg I never heard from them again. So what it ended up being was an all-expense-paid trip to Pat O'Brien's piano bar.

I heard from Tech a little bit here and there during this period. But it was getting late, the end of February or early March, and I kept waiting for them to do something, and they weren't doing anything. I was really disappointed.

I had always wanted to go to Tech. I grew up going to games in Miles Stadium and watching Carroll Dale, Bob Schweickert and Sonny Utz. Boy, they were all great! My uncle, Sharrell Allen, had gone to Tech, and he was a bachelor, and he took me and Barnett to a lot of games. I loved how that cannon fired when Tech scored and how great the Highty-Tighties sounded. I thought Miles Stadium was huge. It's funny, I see pictures of it now, and it seems so small. There were a few bleachers on either side of the press box, and that was it. But it seemed so big then.

The best game I ever saw in Miles Stadium came in 1964. That was when Tech beat No. 10 Florida State, 20-11. FSU wide receiver Fred Biletnikoff was leading the country in receiving but had a tough day. He finally got a touchdown pass late in the game and out of frustration he flung the ball into the stands. The funny thing was that our free safety, John Raible, couldn't raise his arms much past his shoulders. He had both shoulders operated on many years before, and he just couldn't raise them. The following year they moved him to an eight-technique (a Rover or Whip in our defense today). But on that day, here was a guy playing free safety against one of the great passing teams in the country, and he couldn't raise his arms over his head. And Tech beat them!

Now it was getting late in the recruiting process. VMI was showing some interest, so I planned to visit Lexington that weekend. Dad got an extension-course engineering degree from VMI. He was never against Tech; it was more like he was for VMI. He had two brothers who graduated from VMI and one who graduated from Tech. So the family was sort of 50-50 on it. And that was a big game back then, VPI-VMI. They always played on Thanksgiving day in Roanoke, at Victory Stadium. I had an Aunt Hazel who lived in Salem, and we'd all go to her house after the game and you could always feel some tension in the air.

But I knew the military life wasn't for me.

Then, that week, Tech's John Shelton called and offered me

a scholarship. I accepted before he could change his mind.

A few days later they sent Red Laird to my house to get the letter of intent signed.

Now, Red Laird was a legendary coach at Virginia Tech. A legendary BASEBALL coach.

I guess they didn't want one of their football coaches to waste his time on signing this little quarterback from Hillsville. I kind of realized where I stood then. I never took an official visit. They offered me a scholarship over the phone then sent over the baseball coach to sign me.

But I didn't care. I was just glad to have that piece of paper in my hand. I figured, the more time they had to think about it, they more they might try to back out of this deal.

4

I WASN'T BIG, BUT I MADE UP FOR IT BY BEING SLOW

WHEN I ARRIVED in Blacksburg in August of 1965 there were about 60 freshmen and seven of us were quarterbacks. On the first day of practice, the coaching staff took a good look at me.

On the second day of practice, I was in the defensive secondary.

I wasn't exactly dazzling anybody with my athleticism. It's too bad because I had a chance to play in the first game ever at Lane Stadium. It was our freshman team vs. the University of Maryland's freshman team, on a Friday afternoon in 1965. But I didn't play. I stood on the sideline the whole time and watched.

Blacksburg High had a home football game later that night. I was just one year removed from high school, so I was still interested in the game. But I was so embarrassed that I hadn't played that afternoon, I stayed over on the hill the whole game. I wouldn't go sit in the stands where people could see me. I was wondering, "Am I not good enough to play here?" I was so disappointed and depressed. But I worked my way into the next ballgame, and things kind of worked out after that.

Playing defensive back, I wasn't very fast, so I basically played zone coverage. I couldn't play man-to-man. I guess I ran a 4.9. Maybe a 4.88 on a good day. Let's just say I wasn't challenging anybody to race. I didn't need that kind of embarrassment.

But receivers rarely got behind me. I could always feel that inside guy going to the flat and I'd know when the other guy was going to curl up. I always seemed to know what to expect. A lot of people might have caught balls in front of me, but not behind me.

I wasn't a great athlete. I was the holder for extra points, when Jon Utin was the kicker. One week we put in a fake. And I'm excited because, hey, I'm a guy who threw 43 touchdown passes in high school and I'm going to get a chance to maybe throw one in a college game! So when it comes time to run the fake on Saturday, Coach Claiborne turns to our starting quarterback, Al Kincaid.

"Al," he said, "jump in there and run this fake."

Never mind that when the other team saw Al go in there, it would tip off the play. Coach Claiborne wanted Al instead of me. That was the worst insult I ever got. It was a tremendous blow to my ego.

I would never recruit myself today. I remember sitting in a staff room one day in 1987 with assistant coaches Tommy Groom, Larry Creekmore and Duke Strager. All four of us had played here at Tech. We were watching tape of a recruit, and I looked around the room.

"You know, guys, I don't think a one of us could play at this level now," I said. "And I know we couldn't get into school today."

When I played, VMI had this great wideout named Frank Easterly. Remember, back then, Tech was called "VPI," and our big rival was VMI.

One year, VMI had first-and-goal at our five-yard line and Frank ran three straight out-routes against me. VMI was picking on me and Frank was open three consecutive times, but their quarterback overthrew him every time. They had me beat like a drum.

I still joke with Frank about it now. "No way you guys could score against me down there!"

The best player I ever faced was Florida State wide receiver Ron Sellers. He was big and he could run. He tore us up. The first time we faced him he caught about 13 passes on me and our other corner, Ron Davidson.

The next year we went down to Tallahassee. Lenny Smith was our sophomore free safety. It was his first year as a starter. Well, this time, Sellers was having a tough day, and he came across the middle and Smith popped him real good. I saw Lenny getting in Sellers' face a little bit, and it was a race between me and Ron to get to him.

"Don't get this guy irritated," we said. "We know what he can do. He caught about a million passes against us last year. Keep your mouth shut and let a sleeping dog lie!" Lenny got all upset at us, these two seniors telling him to shut up.

Sellers, Easterly, Walker Gillette of Richmond, they were great receivers. I played against our outside linebackers coach, Jim Cavanaugh, too. He was a wideout for William & Mary. He was pretty good. But I still kid him about the time I popped him good.

He had a big game against us the year before, so we wanted to try to do something to get in his head. It was their first passing situation of the game and Jim got down in his three-point stance. He had his head down, watching the snap, and didn't see me take a running start. I timed it perfectly, hitting him full speed when the ball was snapped. I jacked him pretty good. Knocked him back a good five feet. He was quite a bit taller than me, so the whole key was sneaking up on him. I still ride him pretty good about that one.

I was just an average guy on the football team here at Tech. Coach Claiborne discouraged people from being in fraternities, but mostly fraternity people welcomed us at their place, so I ended up going to a lot of fraternity parties. I'd really get upset when these fraternity people would be kind enough to invite us in to their place and about midnight, one of our guys was punching out the president of the fraternity. I couldn't understand that. Here they let us into their house and then all of a sudden one of our guys was punching him out.

Back then, the fraternities were the main deal. There really wasn't a place in downtown Blacksburg for kids to hang out like there is now. But we did have a place called Cecil's on the other end of town. There were two pool tables in there that sort of served two functions. The first was to play pool. The second was a place to hide under when you heard a gun go off.

But I think things have gotten looser today. Back then, if you drank a couple of beers, that was a serious thing.

That gets back to punching out the president of the fraternity. I just don't understand that. Why take your chances of getting your life screwed up and losing your scholarship over a few words at a party? I don't understand it and I don't think I ever will. In our program we talk a lot about avoiding those kinds of situations. I'm realistic about college life, but at the same time, I have certain expectations that our players must uphold.

I played from 1966-68. I got my degree in distributive education. I was team captain as a senior; a member of Omicron Delta Kappa leadership fraternity; was President of the

Monogram Club; was selected to Who's Who in American Colleges and Universities; and made Dean's List.

Lenny Luongo and Ron Davidson were probably my closest friends when I played. But a teammate I will never forget is Frankie Loria.

He was a very quiet guy. He married his wife, Phyllis, while he was in school. He didn't say a lot, but he was one of those guys that if he did say something, you were straining your ear to hear because it must be important.

He played safety and was Tech's first consensus all-American, but he might have trouble playing man coverage in today's schemes. We had a footwork drill in practice where you would step through ropes. You watched him do that drill and your first thought was for his personal safety. He'd be crossing his feet up and trip and fall. He just couldn't get through those ropes.

And he had a hard time back-pedaling. He only ran about a 4.7 in the 40-yard dash, but I tell you, he was quick. He was only about 5-foot-9, weighed 175, but when he hit you it was like a karate chop. He hit people so quick it stunned them. He had huge thighs, which gave him great explosiveness, and he would sting you.

It's funny. He wasn't much of a practice guy. His sole purpose in life was to get through practice. But nobody ever doubted that, when the game started on Saturday, he was ready to go from the first whistle.

He was Marshall's defensive coordinator in 1970 when their plane crashed and everybody on the plane died. I was at Cheryl's parents' home in Richmond when the news came over at 11 p.m. I remember it very clearly. A sickening feeling.

He was 23 years old.

Rick Tolley was also a former Tech player. Class of 1960. And he was the head coach at Marshall, and they had that program going pretty well. It was such an awful tragedy. It still just hurts your stomach when you remember what happened.

Frankie had a real future in coaching. Someone once asked me, "If Frankie Loria was still living, would he be coaching for you?"

"If Frankie was still here," I said, "I might be coaching for him."

Our coach, Jerry Claiborne, was absolutely a no-nonsense guy. A disciplinarian. He had intense eyes, and when he stared at you, well, you didn't want to be on his bad side. Fear was actually involved. You knew he didn't mess around. I mean, 60 freshmen came in with my class, and only 13 were left at the end. So you knew he wouldn't hesitate to get rid of anybody. He was tough, demanding and physical. And he was good.

I always thought he was at his best right after a disappointing loss. That next week, he just had a way of motivating and getting things corrected, so that we were going to be good against that next team.

As players, we all had all special stories about him holding practices on Saturday nights after particularly poor games.

That never happened to us, but we knew it was a possibility. But we had some rough Mondays. There were practices where we didn't execute well. "That was on MY time," he'd say. "Now we're on YOUR time." And he'd make us stay late until we got it right.

As a player, I really believed in him. I feared him. To me, he was the perfect college coach, and I still feel that way.

I remember when we received our first Liberty Bowl invitation in 1966, to play Miami.

"Nobody gets on the plane without a haircut," Coach Claiborne said.

Every single player went and had their hair cut short the way Coach Claiborne liked it.

Going to those bowls back then was a big, big deal. There weren't that many of them, like today. My junior year we were

7-0 and then lost two in a row. Next, we played VMI and lost, 12-10, and were out of contention. It was a real feat to go to two bowls, but we were that close to going to three in a row.

At the first Liberty Bowl the officials gave us these neat dark watches. Every minute, a picture of the Liberty Bowl would appear on the face. It would fade out, then come back. I mean this is quite a big-time watch. We got them at a luncheon and we all put them on. A few minutes passed, and I heard someone say, "Hey, mine just stopped!"

Then a few seconds passed, and someone said, "Hey, MINE just stopped!"

And this went on for four minutes, five minutes, 10 minutes. Everybody yelling, "hey, mine just stopped!" And there were bets going on over who's watch was going to die next.

It was a great idea, but they all quit running. I took mine off and just left it in the case. When I wanted to show it to somebody, I'd wind it up and let it come on. But I wouldn't test it too much.

The other thing I remember about that first bowl was the big crowd at that luncheon, and how Coach Claiborne took control of that whole room when it was his turn to speak. Years later I thought of that, when I had to speak at a similar luncheon for our first bowl, the Independence. Terry Bradshaw was there speaking, too, and I was nervous as heck. I was worried about going up there and botching it, after Coach Claiborne had done such a nice job. But somehow I got through the whole thing and it all worked out.

The second Liberty Bowl (in 1968), we played Ole Miss, who had that great sophomore quarterback, Archie Manning. We jumped out to a 17-0 lead, and that just got them upset. Manning threw two touchdown passes and we lost, 34-17. We kinda got Manning's career going with that game. We got his son Peyton's career at Tennessee started out pretty good 26 years later in the Gator Bowl, so I haven't had much luck with the Manning family.

The thing I remember most about that game was how cold it was. I had gotten the flu and had been in the infirmary a couple of days before we left. I was trying to get my strength back. Now, I have been in many games in Lane Stadium, played in the snow, all kinds of weather, but I've never been as cold as I was that day. I was standing out there in the first quarter actually shivering.

I look back at that Liberty Bowl team my senior year. We weren't very talented. But we were tough. We didn't turn the ball over, we played great defense and we had a strong kicking game. We won a lot of ballgames, but people complained that we were way too conservative.

My first year out of college, I remember going to a game with Cheryl, sitting up in the stands at Lane Stadium, about five rows down from the press box. Some guys in front of me were complaining.

"Claiborne stinks," they said. "He's a lousy coach."

They kept going on and on. "What is he doing? He's awful."

Finally, I couldn't help myself. I leaned down toward them.

"Hey, do you know the guy?" I said. "Do you know what he's trying to do with that particular play? Or are you just running your mouth when you have no idea what you're talking about?"

Finally, Cheryl interrupted us. "Frank, it's time to go."

But I kept on. "Well, I know the guy. I played for him," I said.

I think if Cheryl hadn't been with me, I would have punched one of them right there under the press box. But once they realized I played for Coach Claiborne, they shut up.

Remember, 60 of us were in my recruiting class, and only 13 survived. But those 13 would go up against anyone for Coach Claiborne.

5

GETTING ON WITH MY LIFE'S WORK

WHEN I WAS a player I never thought about being a football coach. As a kid I thought I wanted to be a doctor. I had been around them so much after my accident, and a lot of the family thought that would be my calling.

But then I had finished my senior year and realized I wasn't ready to give up football. That's when I first thought seriously about coaching. I was able to get a job on the staff at nearby Radford High School. That summer, in 1969, I had to come back to Tech to take a couple more math classes so I could teach at Radford.

I'll tell you exactly when I knew my future was in coaching. It was right after I had finished playing, and Bill Brill of The Roanoke Times wrote a column saying how this new local semipro football team, the Roanoke Buckskins, should get some local talent like Frank Beamer and Ron Davidson to create interest and put people in the stands. Now, as slow as I was, I never thought about pro football. But after reading that article, I thought, "Wait a minute. Maybe this is a way I can get back in the game."

I always respected Coach Claiborne's judgment, so I went to him. "Coach," I said, "I read this newspaper article this morning and it got me thinking. Do you reckon I should go up to Roanoke and try to play semipro football?"

He looked at me with those eyes of his.

"Frank, if I were you," he said, "I would get on with my life's work."

I thought, "Get on with my life's work?"

"I don't believe you've got a future in pro football," he said.

I was like, "So, uh, what are you trying to tell me, coach?" He was honest, boy. I'll never forget those words. But it was good advice.

I got on the football staff at Radford High School under Harold Absher, and while there I got my master's degree in guidance at Radford College. Harold retired after one year, and so I applied for the head job. This was my second year out of school. I was probably real close to getting that job, but instead they brought in Norm Lineburg, who went on to become a legend there. At the time I was disappointed, but looking back, it was the best thing that could have happened. I wasn't ready to be a head coach. And if I had, I'm not sure I would have become a graduate assistant coach at Maryland two years later. Things just seemed to work out. I learned a lot under Norm, who is a great coach.

Coach Claiborne got the job at Maryland in 1971. One of my teammates, George Foussekis, was one of the first guys he hired. Well, Radford had just won the state championship and we had some good players. George came down on a recruiting trip and asked me if I'd be interested in coming to College Park as a graduate assistant. I'm not sure, but in the back of his mind, he was probably thinking it would help him sign a few of our players if I was there.

Back then you could have as many graduate assistants as you wanted, and they didn't actually have to take classes. We had five at Maryland. George was honest with me.

"I don't think Coach Claiborne is paying the GA's very much," he said.

"Aw, George, you know I played for him," I said. "Those other GA's, they didn't play for him. He'll take care of me."

"I don't know, Frank," George said. "I think he's only paying them about $150 a month."

"I think he'll do me better," I said.

So I go up there and walk into Coach Claiborne's office and told him I'd like to join the staff as a graduate assistant.

"Well, that's great, Frank," he said. "I can pay you $150 a month."

I was a little taken aback. "Well, Cheryl and I, we're planning on getting married ..."

"Yeah," he said. "I can give you $150 a month."

I was beginning to see that I was going to get $150 a month or nothing. So I took it. But that was Coach Claiborne. He treated everybody the same.

I met my wife, Cheryl, during my senior year at Tech through a blind date sent up by the late Waddey Harvey. I loved Waddey; he was a really good friend. A special guy. He was a great lineman who played in the NFL with the Buffalo Bills. Waddey married Cheryl's sister, Shelia.

It was after a ballgame and we went to a fraternity party. I can't remember which fraternity, but it was a house on Main Street, across from what is now a restaurant called Bogen's. A Wendy's hamburger joint is there now. But that's where we went. We just kind of hung out and got along well.

We started to date some. She would come to visit, but it

always bothered her that I'd rather hang out with the football buddies than do something with her. Or if we did do something, it was always with the football guys. But I think we were fortunate that we met in my senior year. Because that's kind of the way things were; you just hung out with a group of your friends.

We had some arguments here and there because I was always hanging out with my guys — especially Ron Davidson and Lenny Luongo.

Lenny's mom would send down these great meatball sandwiches. Lenny's son later came to Tech and held my headset cord on the sideline for me for several years. And Ron's son came here to play football. Lenny Smith was part of our group, too, and his son Ryan also played for us.

Then there were the married guys, Waddey and Rick Piland. And Jim Pigninelli was in that group a little bit.

Waddey passed away on July 4, 1997. He first started feeling poorly at the 1996 Orange Bowl. He went in for tests. They found he had colon cancer. Waddey got so weak, Lenny Luongo would go over to his house and just get him in the car and ride around, just to get him outside. He died six months after the bowl game.

Two years later, Sheila married Jim Pigninelli. I was glad to see she was able to find someone to enjoy life with. Cheryl and I are very happy for her.

When I met Cheryl, she was working in Richmond. She had gone to Averett College, which was a two-year school at the time, then went to the University of North Carolina at Greensboro for a year before returning home to Richmond.

I really thought she was pretty; I loved it when she pulled her hair back. And she was very down-to-earth, very modest, very caring. She was just perfect for me.

So Cheryl and I got married on April 1, 1972. I was 25 years old, and that summer we went up to Maryland, looking for a place to live. Well, the cost of living up there is a little different than Southwest Virginia. I was making $150 a month and I couldn't find anything decent that we could afford.

Finally I found a one-bedroom apartment out at Spring Hill Lakes, right off the Beltway. It was a nice, safe area. But it cost $190 a month. I filled out the form anyway:

OCCUPATION: Graduate Assistant Football Coach, University of Maryland.
SALARY: $150 a month.

Right there on the form, it said the rent was $190 a month. I handed the lady the application and she looked it over. You should have seen the look on her face. She peered up at me over her reading glasses.

"This isn't going to work," she said.

"You don't understand," I said. "My wife is going to get a job; we're going to be all right. I'm sure she is going to be able to find a job around here somewhere."

She shook her head. "No," she said. "This isn't going to work."

Fortunately Cheryl's parents were waiting out in the car. I said, "What if my wife's parents co-sign this thing? Can we get it then?"

So they co-signed it and we got that $190 one-bedroom apartment even though I was making $150 a month.

We had quite a few graduate assistants at Maryland, and it was kinda difficult keeping us all busy. The first game of the season we played North Carolina. We had a field house in one end zone and there was a scoreboard on top of it.

Assistant coach Jerry Eisman said, "We want one of you guys to go up there on top of the scoreboard with a pair of binoculars. We want you to tell us whether Carolina's defensive tackle is a five technique, outside shade, or head-up in a four.

We need to know what that defensive tackle is doing."

This was my first college game assignment and I was very excited I had a head set and microphone — the whole deal. Carolina lined up on defense, and I looked at the tackle, and said, "He's in a five. He's in a five."

On the other end, I heard, "OK." This went on for about two series.

"He's in a four," I said on the third series. But I didn't hear anything on the other line.

"He's in a four. A four," I repeated.

Nothing.

I figured they must have just gotten off the line for a play. So on the next play, I say, "he's in a five this time. A five."

Again, no answer. I did this about four or five more times and realized the microphone wasn't working. So I set my headset down and watched the game. I was so disappointed; I felt like I wasn't contributing at all.

That night I told Cheryl, "I'm not going to be sitting up on that scoreboard doing nothing for very long."

But later on that year they assigned me the Clemson scouting report. I went down there and saw Clemson play North Carolina on Saturday and I knew this was my big chance. I was supposed to present it to the coaching staff Sunday night. Man,

I really worked on that thing. I had everything there was to know about Clemson in there. How much Gatorade they drank on the sideline. Everything. Maybe that made an impression, because when Bobby Ross, our linebackers coach, got the Citadel head coaching job in 1973, he hired me.

Now I was a full-time assistant football coach.

6

THE INFLUENCE OF BOBBY ROSS

THE CITADEL was a great starting point for me. This was a time, in the early 1970's, right after the Vietnam War, when it wasn't "cool" to be in the military. So trying to recruit high school kids was tough. And the ones we did get might not have been as talented as some others. The situation really forced us to be good teachers.

But the best thing of all: I was making more than $150 a month.

Cheryl and I were very happy there. I liked working with Bobby Ross, I liked our players. It was a good community. My son, Shane, was born March 31, 1977; the year I was named defensive coordinator at The Citadel. It was a great place to raise a son. It was safe, and I can't tell you how many hours Cheryl logged, pushing Shane around in that little buggy every day.

We had a great staff. Bobby would later win a national championship at Georgia Tech in 1990 and is now the head coach of the Detroit Lions. Defensive line coach Ralph Friedgen was the offensive coordinator for the San Diego Chargers and is now a respected offensive coordinator at Georgia Tech. Quarterbacks/wide receivers coach Jimmye Laycock has been head coach at William & Mary for 20 years. Running backs coach Cal McCombs is head coach at VMI. Linebackers coach Charlie Rizzo is an assistant at Rice. Rusty Hamilton coached the offensive line and I coached the defensive backs.

That's three head coaches from one group of assistants that Bobby had at Maryland.

Even though I was a defensive coach, it was at The Citadel where I got my offensive philosophy.

We were in a preseason meeting talking about what we wanted to teach the kids. I was explaining a coverage, one I knew extremely well.

Bobby believed you had to open up the field.

He was such a detail-oriented guy and he instilled that in his assistants.

"But Frank," Bobby said, "what if two receivers get over here, and they're split a certain distance apart?"

"Well, I'd probably adjust this guy out a little bit," I said.

"How much?"

So on a diagram, I showed him. "About this much," I said.

"No," he said. "Exactly how many yards?"

I couldn't say for sure.

"After we meet back after lunch today, I want you to tell me how much," he said. "I want to know exactly what you're saying."

That's what I needed at the time. I knew what I meant, but as a coach, you can't just round off a number. You need to be very exact. If you mean "two-and-a-half yards," then you don't say, "a couple of steps." He made me become a detailed guy.

We still keep in touch. We talk when we need to talk. It's not like we call every month, but if there's something going on I need advice on, I'll call him. After that 2-8-1 season in 1992, he was one of the first people I visited.

He's one of the most genuine, caring people you could ever imagine. And a good coach. He could talk to you about offense, defense, special teams. He left The Citadel to coach the Kansas City Chiefs' special teams.

When the Chiefs later named him as running backs coach, the Chiefs interviewed me to replace him. Marv Levy was the head coach there at the time, and I was still an assistant at Murray State. That job went to Don Lawrence, who is still is coaching in the NFL. Again, things kind of worked out, because if I had gone to the pros, you just don't know how that would have gone.

Instead I stayed at Murray State and was later named the head coach there.

And when the Packers wanted to talk about me being their coach in January (2000), I called Bobby to talk about that. I was interested in the Packers job because of the organization. That's the one pro team where the atmosphere is a lot like college.

I also have a great deal of respect for general manager Ron Wolf. He's an impressive guy. So there were some things that were very attractive about that situation. I was flattered they were interested. But I didn't feel like the timing was right for me to pursue it. There are good things at every level, and there are problems at every level. But I really believe college football is where I belong.

But I talked to Bobby about the situation. I know there are some things he misses about the college game. He likes seeing kids develop, and he misses that. But there are certain things he likes about the pro level. Of course, one is that they pay so well. Of course, he's never been a guy about money. That's never going to be the bottom line with him.

As head coach at Detroit and being in the same division, he knows a lot about Green Bay from a personnel standpoint, from an organizational standpoint, from an ownership standpoint, from a lot of different standpoints. He thought that if I was going to go in that direction, Green Bay would be a good coaching position.

I asked him about the biggest differences between the college and pro game.

"In the NFL, you really need to define what your responsibilities are, and what are the responsibilities of the general manager," he said. "And what kind of involvement you're going to have with the salary cap.

"Professional football is more of a 'me' game instead of a 'we' game. That's nobody's fault, it's just the nature of the game's structure."

Virginia Tech would be a tough place for me to leave for a lot of different reasons.

Most importantly, the program is changing, and how people perceive our program is changing. At a lot of places, maybe you're continuing the previous success, but you're not changing anything. At Green Bay, the best you could do would be what a couple of guys had already done — like Lombardi and Holmgren did in winning Super Bowls — and you're just trying to get back to that level.

Here at Virginia Tech, we've moved the program into a new way of thinking. And when you look back on it one day, you feel like you've made a difference. So it would be hard for me to leave here.

It's funny; I wasn't really looking to leave The Citadel. We were very happy there. It was 1977, and Bobby had left. I was the defensive coordinator and thought I had a shot at the head coaching job, but they gave it to Art Baker. Again, things worked out, because with the situation at The Citadel, the question always is, how many games can you win?

Well, that season Ron Zook — my first defensive coordinator on my staff at Tech — was a graduate assistant at Murray State under Mike Gottfried. Mike wanted to play the eight-man front. Coach Claiborne was now at Kentucky and Mike got to know some of the guys on the staff, who knew me. So he would call from time to time, asking questions about the eight-man front. After that season they were looking for a defensive coordinator, and they called me and asked for suggestions. I didn't know Murray State from whatever, but I went around our staff, asking a couple of guys if they would be interested in the job.

A short time later, Ron Zook came out and spent four or five days with me. We talked defense, and he finally convinced me that I should come out and at least visit the place. I went out there and was amazed at Murray State's facilities. It's a small town, but a lot like Blacksburg.

I called Cheryl. "I think I kind of like this place," I told her.

And with each phone call, I got to liking it more and more. Everything was centered around the university. It was a friendly community. Some of my best friends still live there. The place reminded me so much of Blacksburg. Murray is in the southwest part of Kentucky; Blacksburg is in the southwest part of Virginia. Both places have lakes. In both places, I lived about eight minutes from work and drove past a golf course to get there, so I kind of liked that.

And I really liked Mike Gottfried. And I really got the idea from the university officials that they were committed to doing things right.

The move just seemed right.

7

OUR SPECIAL TEAMS BEGAN AT MURRAY STATE

I WAS DEFENSIVE coordinator at Murray State from 1979-80, and when Mike Gottfried went to the University of Cincinnati in 1981, they named me head coach.

I was 34 years old.

That was quite a year. I became a head coach for the first time. Then, on May 6, 1981, our daughter, Casey, was born.

Although I was young, there was never any question in my mind that I was ready. And I had a great staff: Mike O'Cain, who later became head coach at North Carolina State, was my offensive coordinator. Ralph Friedgen was my assistant head coach. Bud Foster, our defensive coordinator here at Tech, was a graduate assistant.

From 1981-86 we went 42-23-2 and were Ohio Valley co-champions my last year. From 1984-85 we stayed in the Top 20 of Division I-AA for 22 consecutive weeks, and my Racer teams finished higher than selected in conference standings five out of those six years.

The secrets to our success then are the same as they are now. Treat people right, work hard, communicate with your players. My door was always open then and it's always open now. Some coaches require an appointment for a player to talk to him. I have never been that way. I just think that if you need to talk, let's talk.

The other thing that I have always believed in are strong special teams.

My special teams at Murray State blocked 34 kicks in six years, almost six a season. And we've received national acclaim for our ability to block kicks at Virginia Tech.

In the 1990's, we blocked 63 kicks, more than any other Division I-A program in the 1990's. We blocked 31 punts, 18 PAT's and 14 field goals.

There is no secret to our success. It's a combination of good planning and hard work.

It used to be that each one of our coaches was in charge of one of the special teams. So there was a period on Sunday where they had to grade the film and get the special teams ready for next week. That was time they could have been working on offense or defense.

Instead, now Billy Hite coaches the kickoff return team, Bud Foster coaches the field goal block team, Bryan Stinespring coaches the field goal protection team and I coach everything else: punt block return, kickoff coverage and punt protection teams.

Plus I do all the grading and planning, which frees them up. And I spend a lot more time on it than they probably would. I easily spend four hours a week alone just preparing for the punt-block and return teams.

I study everything the other team does, looking for an

advantage. How much spacing there is between blockers? Anything. I just keep staring until I find something. You wouldn't expect, say, your defensive backs coach to spend four hours on that and then get into his defense. I firmly believe this is the most efficient way to operate.

It's not hard to find someone who wants to run your offense or defense. Finding the RIGHT guy might be an issue, but everybody comes in familiar with either offense or defense. Now, when the head coach gets involved in that area, he's taking over something most coaches don't want to mess with. An added bonus to that, you see, is that you lend credibility to it. If the players see that the head coach believes special teams are so important that he coaches them personally, then it makes them indeed "special."

Everybody acknowledges that special teams plays are one-third of football, but few actually treat it that way. If anything, it might be more important than one-third, because they are usually big-yardage plays, big momentum plays, plays that can quickly affect the score. So when the kids see me involved in special teams, they know they're important.

Also, I've always put my best athletes on special teams. It takes a player with good hand-eye coordination to block a kick. And it takes skill to block somebody in the open field. You can't be a slug. You must have good football awareness and react quickly, because things are going full-speed.

I tell my defensive coaches, "You give me about two or three weeks watching a guy on a kickoff, and I'll tell you if he's going to be a good defensive player for us." I can just tell by the way he reacts to blocks, and how he hits people, and how he runs people down, and how he squares up against someone. It all calls for great athletic ability and good football sense.

Here's another thing. If you are ever hiring coaches, if you can, try to hire a guy who has special teams experience. On our staff now, Jim Cavanaugh did it at North Carolina, Danny

Pearman did it at Alabama, and Billy Hite and Bud Foster have done it for years here at Tech.

We hold personnel meetings, discussing who would be good on kickoff coverage or punt block teams. That's where Billy Hite might say, "one of my fullbacks, Wayne Ward, would be really good in that situation." So we gave him a shot, and he was terrific.

That's how we ended up with the 1999 Big East Defensive Player of the Year, Corey Moore, playing special teams. A guy like Corey, or LaVar Arrington at Penn State, might not block every kick, but they're occupying people, and they might free someone else to block the kick.

The keys are putting good athletes on special teams and making them important. I don't think we spend more time on it than most other schools. But I do think we make it more important.

I would never ask a special teams guy to come early before practice or stay late after practice.

When you do that, you're doing two things.

No. 1, you are asking a punt-block guy to spend more time on the field than his teammates. Now, in a sense, he thinks he's getting punished, so he's not going to be as enthused about being on the special teams. And then, of course, he won't play as well.

And No. 2, you're sending out the message that special teams aren't important enough to be done during the regular practice hours. So then you have two things working against you. We never do that. We do all of our special teams work during the regular practice.

Our practices move. There isn't much standing around. But our kicking period is the one time we bring everybody together. This sends out the message that this is important. For us to stop here in the middle of everything and work on this, it is important. Their teammates are standing and watching the special teams guys perform. Yes, you have players standing around, but I think in this case, it's worth it.

We probably don't spend more practice time on special teams than anybody else. The one area we might spend a little more time than most people is blocking kicks. We work on it Mondays, Wednesdays and Thursdays, a total of about 20 minutes for the week. We do it fast. But I don't know that most programs in the country would actually practice blocking kicks 20 minutes a week. Because there are so many other aspects to special teams: returning punts, returning kickoffs, covering kickoffs, field goals, the whole thing.

But I think it is time well-spent. It is physically difficult to block a kick. Things happen so fast back there, and a guy has to be comfortable with his landmark, how to stay in control and take the ball off the punter's foot. The more you do it in practice, the more likely it will happen on Saturday. If you've only done it once, if you break through, all of a sudden you're back there and you might overrun the ball, or you might rough the kicker, any number of things, because you're in unfamiliar territory.

On top of all that, I spend a good four hours Sunday and Monday just putting together a game plan for a punt block and a punt return. And then, all week, I'm studying more video.

I try to come up with one new rush every week. I think we were one of the first teams to take people off the headhunters. The headhunters are the two wide guys in a punting team formation.

The theory was, you would guard them, because if you didn't, the punter or the up-back could throw it to them because they'd be wide open. Then you get into the issue of whether that passer can react in time, and accurately get the ball to the headhunter, and the headhunter actually catching it. On top of that, if you're at your own 30, that takes a lot of guts to throw the ball and risk an incompletion, because now the other team takes over on downs.

So we decided to bring the two guys off the headhunter, and now we had two fast people coming at the kicker who were unaccounted for. But then we'd bring another guy back out, trying to confuse things. It was kind of a different concept, but now a lot of teams do it.

Here's another thing, and it gets back to those years playing Florida State in Tallahassee. In 1988, I'll never forget, we were deep in our own territory and they had Deion Sanders back to return the kick, and their crowd was worked up into a frenzy. Just screaming their lungs out.

We didn't really want to kick it to Deion, because he was so great at returning kicks, and has continued to do that in the NFL. And they had all those fast guys up front who could block the kick.

So we had some fakes put in and called them twice. One time the personal protector didn't hear it, and another time the center didn't hear it. It was too loud and things got all screwed up.

But that always made an impression on me that the better you can block a kick, the better your chances are to return a kick. You wanted to protect your kicker against the block, but if you stayed in there too long, Deion was going to return it on you. And then there was the crowd on top of that.

To me, the punt returner is like your quarterback. Once you find him, you don't change him. The toughest thing to do in football is return punts. You've got to catch a very high ball with people bearing down on you. And the player has got to want to do it, too. That kind of guy just doesn't come around all the time. The 1999 season, we were lucky. We had two good ones in Ricky Hall and Ike Charlton.

I haven't changed a lot since my days at Murray State. I've learned some things about organizing a practice, and I delegate authority much more.

I learned that after that 2-8-1 season in 1992. I was stretching myself too thin. I was into everything. I ran an offensive meeting, and we'd be ready to make a decision, and my phone would ring. It would be an important call, so I'd have to take it, then all of a sudden all those guys in that offensive meeting are sitting around waiting on me. It was not a good use of time.

Today, I firmly believe that you hire people in whom you have great confidence and you let them do their job. If there's a problem, you talk to them about it, but it's their job.

Those Murray State years were something. It was a great place, but we just didn't have the money of the Big I-A programs.

In 1982, Morehead State upset us, 13-10, and we faced a six-hour bus ride back home. We stopped at a Kentucky Fried Chicken to eat on the way back, and our order wasn't ready. We had a bus full of hungry players and we wanted to get home. So my assistants and I got off the bus and helped get things going. The KFC people cooked and we boxed it up.

Finally, we got all of our kids fed. We were sweating and tired. We were in the midst of a 4-7 season and now this. I looked at my assistants. I was not a happy guy.

"You guys hungry?" I said.

They looked around at each other. "No, coach," Bud Foster said.

"Me neither. Let's go."

We rode six hours back to Murray on empty stomachs. Later, Bud told me he had never been so hungry in his entire life.

We rode a lot of busses at Murray. There was one ride my son, Shane, remembers more than the others. In was 1985 and we were playing Eastern Kentucky for the conference championship. He went along for the trip and was very excited about it.

He and Cheryl were at the hotel, which had a video game

61

arcade. Some of our players were in there playing, killing time before the bus left for the stadium. "Mom, I'll meet you on the bus," he said, and went inside.

"The bus leaves in 20 minutes," Cheryl said. "Don't be late. You know your dad doesn't tolerate tardiness."

Shane said OK. He started playing and got caught up in the game. When he finally looked up, the arcade was empty.

Everybody was on the bus. It was time to go. "Where's Shane?" I said.

Our quarterback, Kevin Sisk, came up from the back of the bus.

"Last I saw him, he was in the video game arcade," he said.

"Go get him," I said.

Kevin returned with Shane, who acted like nothing was the matter. As soon as he came up the steps, I grabbed him by the collar and jerked him down in the seat between me and Cheryl. I might have embarrassed him in front of the team, but you know what?

He was never late for the bus again.

We didn't have a big equipment budget at Murray State. We only had but a certain number of the good football shoes, so we had to save them for our starters. Our equipment manager, Lowell Key, was a really nice guy, though, and sometimes he'd give out a pair of expensive shoes to a player if that player was nice to him.

I walked out to practice one day and there was the kid who hadn't played a down for us all year, and he was wearing the good shoes. I made him take them off right there on the field.

Same thing with our knee braces. Everybody had to wear them in practice, and some of the braces were newer and nicer than others. If a player had a really good practice, he earned the right to wear the best brace.

I wasn't trying to be cruel; we just had limited equipment. But I guess it sort of served as a motivational thing, too.

8

A DREAM
COME TRUE

B O B B Y R O S S could have been the head coach at
Virginia Tech instead of me.

Bobby had resigned from Maryland shortly after the 1986
season ended.

Why? He couldn't get anybody at Maryland to tell him
which way the program was headed. He had questions about
academic requirements, facilities, many things. On Saturday,
after the Terrapins had beaten Virginia in Charlottesville, he
talked with his family on the three-hour drive back to College
Park. That's when he made the decision to resign.

Shortly thereafter, on Friday, December 12, 1986, Virginia
Tech named its new athletic director, Dutch Baughman. That
afternoon Dutch called me. He was looking for a replacement
for outgoing Tech head coach Bill Dooley.

I had already applied for the Virginia Tech job. It was nothing against Murray State, but I knew I wanted to get to a Division I-A school. I always thought, though, that I'd make the move to a lower-end Division I-A school, and then get the big job. And all of a sudden here was Virginia Tech calling.

Dutch had also called Bobby. "Everything is happening too fast," he told Dutch. "I just don't know." In that conversation he had casually mentioned my name to Dutch, who kind of smiled, since I was already on his list.

"Here's my number in case you change your mind," Dutch said.

Dutch was moving quickly and had already narrowed his list to four or five, including me. A few days later I met with him at the Opryland Hotel in Nashville. The interview began at 2 p.m. and went to 6 p.m. and we immediately hit it off. It was as if we were old friends. "I'm going to leave ya'll to talk," Cheryl said. "I'm going shopping."

She rejoined us for dinner then went back to the room. Dutch and I met for about three more hours that night. When I got back to the hotel room I told Cheryl, "I really believe he's going to offer me this job."

In the meantime, Bobby thought things over and called Dutch back. They met in Richmond for five or six hours, and he began to reconsider a little bit. Dutch conducts exhaustive interviews, and he always asks about prospective assistants. He wants to know what guys you're thinking of hiring. Bobby said the first person he would hire would be me. "I'd try my best to get him as my as assistant head coach," he said.

When the meeting was over, Bobby was still mulling over his options. He had interviewed with the University of California and the University of Arizona. He was also considering the NFL; Marv Levy had offered him a job as the passing coordinator for the Buffalo Bills.

After a few days, Dutch called Bobby back to find out

where he stood. His wife, Alice, answered the phone. She told him, "You're crazy if you don't hire Frank."

Dutch then called me and said he'd like to invite me to campus and meet with the university officials. They had to approve me. What he was pretty much telling me was that I had the job unless I screwed things up.

Afterward, Bobby called me. He had changed his mind. His mother was in poor health, and he decided he wanted to stay in the area. He eventually wants to retire to Virginia, you see, so I think he began to feel Virginia Tech might be a good option after all.

"Frankie," he said, "I'm thinking about taking this Virginia Tech job. But before I call Dutch, I need to know if you will join me as assistant head coach."

I was a little taken aback. I didn't know if I should tell him what was happening or not. We're like brothers, so I told him, "sure, I'll support you in whatever you want me to do. I'd be honored to join your staff."

So then I called Dutch and told him about this situation. "No, I've invited you to campus," he said. "You're the guy I want the university officials to meet."

So I called Bobby back. All this took place in the span of about 20 minutes.

"Listen, I've got to tell you this," I said. "Dutch told me he's bringing me to Blacksburg to meet with the school officials."

"Well," he said. "If that's the case, then I'm going to get out of it. I want you to have that job."

Just like that, the picture was clear. Bobby was no longer a candidate. And Dutch emphasized to me that if I accepted his invitation to Blacksburg and everything went well, it meant I was taking the job. There was none of this "let me look around" stuff. He wanted me to be prepared to conduct a press conference.

It was funny; here were the two finalists for this job, and

they're both supporting each other. His wife was telling the AD to hire me; I was telling Bobby I would join him as his assistant; and then Bobby pulled out because he didn't want to stand in my way. All the candor, humor and goodwill that went on in that whole hiring process was really remarkable.

As it turned out, Georgia Tech hired Bobby less than two weeks later, on Jan. 5, and he won a national championship there in 1990.

I don't think I would have been considered for the Tech job if it wasn't for Dutch and then-university president Dr. William Lavery, who was a little bit familiar with me because I was a Tech guy. I know there were a lot of people involved, but if it hadn't been for them, I don't think I would have been hired. I read where they had looked at something like 75 candidates and had narrowed the list down to five. I think Dutch was kinda looking for a Tech guy.

And, to be honest, with all the financial problems they were experiencing at the time, I think they thought they could get me pretty cheap.

So I had that going for me.

But there still wasn't cause for celebration, because I still had to be approved by the board at Virginia Tech. Instead of drinking champagne, I packed my bags for Blacksburg.

You have to understand the climate at Virginia Tech at that time. Dooley had been the coach and athletic director. The university officials wanted to keep him on as coach, but they wanted someone else as the AD. The way I understand it, they had a disagreement there and came to a financial settlement.

And then they hired Dutch. He was something, now. Wore cowboy boots every day to work. Loved farming, animals. He was a really neat guy, down-to-earth. Today, he is the executive director of Division I-A athletic directors and lives just outside of Fort Worth, Texas.

The board unanimously approved me, and Dutch made it

official over dinner at The Farmhouse restaurant in Christiansburg on Dec. 22, 1986. I was 40 years old and the new head coach at my alma mater. He scheduled a press conference for the following day.

I woke up the next morning and felt pretty good until I read the Roanoke newspaper. This was two days before Christmas, and sports columnist Bill Brill found out about the decision. He wrote that Tech naming me as head coach "was kind of like the kid waking up Christmas morning expecting the latest in toys and instead getting a sweater."

Cheryl was really upset when she read that. She was ready to fight. But my response was, "Maybe that kid needs a sweater."

I understood what Brill was saying, because Steve Spurrier's name was mentioned for the job, and Bobby Ross' name was mentioned, and they had bigger names.

I got along fine with Brill, who is retired and now lives in North Carolina.

One summer there was a media gathering up at the Homestead resort and we had a great time. Brill and Bill Millsaps of the Richmond paper, the two veteran sports editors, were there. We had a few drinks and had some great conversations. I ended up riding home with Brill. On the way he made it very apparent he wasn't a Virginia Tech guy. He was an ACC guy. And I understood that. I kind of knew where he was coming from. I didn't try to convince him that he was wrong in his opinion, but I wanted to make sure he knew where I was coming from, too.

Let me tell you, it felt pretty doggone good to get the job. I said it at the time: "This is a dream come true."

I remember that first press conference. I made this comment:

"I think we have the opportunity to win the national championship here. Sure, things have to happen right for you, but I think you have to think big for big things to happen. Look at Miami before Jim Kelly got there. Their program was floundering, and now they're playing for the championship.

"We've already got a winning tradition at Tech. Now we want to continue to build on that tradition, and just get better and better and better."

A lot of people probably thought I was crazy when I said that, or maybe thought I was caught up in naive optimism. My brother, Barnett, was one of them.

He was elated when I got the job, because he didn't think I had much of a chance. But when he heard me up there at the podium talking about a "national championship," he thought I was crazy.

"We're Virginia Tech," he said. "All we want is a winning record, and go to a bowl every three or four years. A national championship? This guy is nuts!"

And that might have been so. I know I received quite a jolt my first week on the job, and Dutch came into my office.

"We're having lunch today with the Deans," he said.

I said, "Hey, great!"

We went over to Hillcrest, which was the athletic dorm at the time, to meet them for lunch and went through the buffet line. There were maybe 20 people in this room. We sat down and I had my salad. Just my salad; I was going to go back and get my main course.

I started to take my first bite, and that's when they started telling me everything that was wrong with the football system at Virginia Tech — how academics were out of whack, everything.

I promise you, this went on for 20 minutes, and I'm still sitting there holding my fork with the lettuce hanging from it, waiting to take my first bite — and never took it.

When I finally got a chance to talk, I said, "we're not on opposite sides of the fence here. We're on the same team. I want to work with you to make sure we do things right."

That was a real eye-opening experience. I didn't realize there was so much bitterness there, but let me tell you, I like Bill Dooley. To me, he did a lot of good things for Virginia Tech. You won't hear me say bad stuff about him.

I don't think the impact of what had happened hit me until a few weeks later. I was at a Hokies' basketball game in Cassell Coliseum, standing up in the opening near the Bowman Club, and I heard the band break into "Tech Triumph," and it gave me chills down my back. That's when it sorta hit me.

My family was excited about my return home, but they were worried, too. Most of the time when you take a new job, the old guy was unsuccessful. But here I was coming into a situation where the old guy, Bill Dooley, had been very, very successful. My brother, Barnett, understood that, and I think he knew there were going to be some problems ahead.

He was right.

9

AND THEN REALITY SET IN

WHEN I WAS putting together my staff I wanted to hire people I was familiar with, and I wanted to also hire Tech people. And I wanted to keep at least one guy from the previous staff, to make the transition easier.

I talked to a lot of people who, asking who should stay, and Billy Hite and Pat Watson's name kept popping up. Pat went to Georgia Tech to work on Bobby Ross' staff. But Billy stayed and he coached the running backs.

I brought in five guys with me from Murray State. They were:

Offensive line and tight ends coach Steve Marshall.
Outside linebackers coach Keith Jones.
Defensive ends coach Duke Strager, a former Hokie teammate.

Defensive tackles coach Larry Creekmore, another former Hokie player.

Inside linebackers coach Bud Foster, who played at Murray.

I also hired quarterbacks coach Rickey Bustle; wide receivers coach Tommy Groom, a former Hokie player (Class of '66) who was assistant head coach at Brown; and assistant head coach and defensive coordinator Ron Zook, who was the defensive secondary coach at Tennessee, and who helped me get on at Murray State.

Rickey Bustle had been working at Murray State with me for free. Prior to that, he had been working for the Arizona Wranglers of the USFL, and that league folded. He knew Mike O'Cain from their Clemson days, so he came to us and worked for nothing until something came up. I couldn't pay him.

Finally, he got offered a job at Austin Peay and went over there. They were going to pay him money! We were giving him nothing at Murray State! And then something happened there that he just didn't like, so he called me up and said, "can I come back?"

I said, "Why not? We're not paying you anything. SURE you can come back!"

So that was my staff. And remember, we were coming into one of the toughest situations a new staff could come in to — replacing a staff that had won. Dooley had just gone 9-2-1 (10-1-1 if you count the Temple forfeit) and won the Peach Bowl. The players rallied behind Dooley and his staff. They loved him, which I fully understood. And here we come in, with everyone expecting us to win. And we might have been OK if we hadn't had so many guys hurt or ruled ineligible.

We got a late start on recruiting that year. It was January of 1987, and we were trying to salvage our first recruiting class. Billy Hite was from DeMatha and had a great relationship with Bill McGregor. We were recruiting two of his players, Jon

Jeffries and Jay Foran. Billy called McGregor and said I was coming up to meet him. It was my first trip up to Northern Virginia for recruiting.

It was morning and we were in Billy's dealer car, on our way to Hyattsville, Md., and we stopped at a 7-Eleven. Both of us got a large 20-ounce cup of coffee. Then we were back on our way. Shortly afterward, Billy came to an intersection and this other guy ran his stop sign. Billy hit his brakes and threw the steering wheel as hard as it could to the right to avoid a collision. My coffee flew everywhere; it went up in the car's cassette player, dashboard, air conditioning vent, all over the place.

Billy's coffee went all over me.

And here I was, trying to make a good first impression with McGregor, soaked in coffee.

Billy joked later that everybody thought I got my burns when I was a child, but it actually happened in his car that morning.

With such a late start, our recruiting went surprisingly good that first year. Five guys from that class were taken in the 1992 NFL Draft. They were offensive tackle Eugene Chung, in the first round by New England; quarterback Will Furrer, in the fourth round by Chicago; safety Damien Russell, in the sixth round by San Francisco; offensive guard William Boatwright, in the seventh round by Philadelphia; and defensive back John Granby, twelfth round, by Denver. Receiver Nick Cullen and tight end Greg Daniels also signed with the Eagles. And tailback Jon Jeffries might have had a pro career if weren't for his injuries.

We redshirted most of those guys, however, and as I went into my first game as Tech's head coach on Sept. 12, 1987, in Lane Stadium, we were without flanker David Everett, linebackers Lawrence White and Jamel Agemy and guard Stacy Johnson, because of injuries. Tailback Tyrone Branch was ruled ineligible. Offensive lineman Jimmy Bryson, safety Derrick Hallman, star defensive tackle Horacio Moronta, cornerback Mitch Dove and linebacker Sean Lucas were academic casualties. We lost, 22-10, to Clemson in front of 42,000 fans in a drenching rain.

It was not the debut I was looking for.

We had lost so many kids that first season, I remember there for a while I dreaded waking up in the morning, because I knew there was going to be something bad happening that day.

What made it worse was watching last year's game film, and seeing all these guys make plays. It brought a little bit more pain to the whole situation. That guy's hurt, that guy's ineligible ... If it could go wrong, it did go wrong there for awhile.

I didn't get my first win until Oct. 3rd. It was a 31-11 win over Navy in Lane Stadium. My shoulders felt a little lighter after that one, but the good feeling didn't last.

Then on Monday, Oct. 26th, the NCAA handed down sanctions incurred during the previous regime: a two-year probation, and for the next three seasons that followed — through 1991 — no more than 85 student-athletes may be on scholarship at any one time.

At that time, you could have 95. Also, we could offer no more than 17 scholarships in 1988-89, while other schools could offer 30.

So in the end that was 33 guys we couldn't recruit in those first couple of years. That really affects you a few years down the road. That hits you in the heart and soul of your program.

"I was surprised by the number of scholarships taken away by the NCAA," I said then. "And I thought the penalty was unfair to me because I was not involved in any of the violations that occurred. But we are going to move forward with out program and get this behind us. With the limitations that we have in recruiting, it was essential now that we go out and get the outstanding athletes, the ones who can contribute to our program."

I knew there were some uncertainties about the program when I took the job, but I'm not sure I thought there would be an investigation or a NCAA ruling. Dutch was very up-front with me as he could be, but I never expected scholarship limitations.

Don't get me wrong, had I known, I still would have taken the job. I mean, how many jobs out there are you going to get? Remember, at Murray State I applied for a lot of jobs and never received a lot of response back. So you take your chances. But it was tough.

On top of that, we had increased academic standards. And it cost us Herman Moore, a great, great wide receiver who signed with Virginia and went on to become a great pro with the Detroit Lions. He was the toughest guy to lose because he wanted to come to Virginia Tech. At least that was his position that last Saturday before signing day, which was on Wednesday. I don't want to make it sound like something it's not. But he told us that day he wanted to go to Virginia Tech.

He was one of those guys who was tough, from an area — Danville —where kids had predominantly gone to Virginia Tech.

Then on Wednesday morning of signing day, it came out in the Richmond paper that one of our school officials, Bud Robertson, was quoted as saying we were no longer accepting partial qualifiers.

A little later I get a call from Herman's high school coach.

Someone had called and told him about the story in the Richmond paper. He wanted to know what we were going to do if he didn't make his SAT scores. Herman had a good grade-point average; he just had not quite made his test scores.

My response was, "Well, he's going to make it. He's just a little bit away."

"But what if he doesn't make it?" he asked.

I then offered, "Let me call the admissions people to see if they will make an exception to the new academic policy."

They were not taking partial qualifiers.

I then told them, "trust me, he's going to make it." But that was the climate at the time.

So Virginia guaranteed his admission, and we could not.

Virginia's coaches were smart. They went down there to Danville on signing day and said, "if you don't sign today, we're withdrawing the offer." Well, he had no choice.

And I remember telling people, "This guy is going to come back and pound Virginia Tech. This guy can really play, and he's going to end up making it."

And he did. He had monster games against us.

I think it affected some recruits after that, because he was from an area we had controlled. And now Virginia was in there.

And then, on top of the scholarship cutbacks and stricter entrance requirements, we faced an upgraded schedule.

I think I realized then that there were a lot of things that had to smooth out. I wanted the job so bad, I would have accepted it no matter what, but I began to realize we were operating in a hole.

The key was to be successful enough to get past all of this. But there were a couple of times when I thought, "This thing might be tough to solve."

10

TRYING TO
TURN IT AROUND

LET ME TELL YOU, those first two years were tough. We won five games and lost 17, and every game was a struggle.

We were kind of walking a tightrope that first year, 1987, when we went 2-9.

We had a group of players who had been successful under Bill Dooley, and now we're having trouble winning football games, and we were trying to keep things from exploding and getting ugly.

I think we put up with some stuff that we wouldn't have otherwise. Kids coming in late for meetings, that kind of stuff. If these players had been successful with us, we would have handled it differently.

As it was we wanted to get through the thing without it exploding. We got through it, but when you're undisciplined

OFF the field, you are going to be undisciplined ON the field.

It was tough. I'd lay there in bed at night and wonder what I should do. I had always been in disciplined programs, from Coach Claiborne to Bobby Ross to Mike Gottfried. There wasn't a lot crap going on in those programs. And here I was trying to walk a thin line.

It boiled over on Nov. 7, 1987, in a 28-16 loss to West Virginia. After the game I complained about our team's lack of discipline. But I blamed myself, not the players.

"It's important that we have a disciplined program," I told reporters. "If you're late for a meeting, or miss curfew, I think it carries over onto the field. We've had too many mistakes, too many breakdowns. It all points to a lack of discipline."

That Monday, I met with every player on our team, letting them air out their feelings.

I talked to offensive guard Kevin Keeffe, one of our seniors. I knew he would speak for most of the players, so I asked him if he had a problem with the team rules.

"The rules are fine," he said. "They just need to be enforced."

I remember what one of our outside linebackers, Jock Jones, said.

"Some nights the coaches checked for curfew and sometimes they didn't," he said. "If someone was late for a meeting, they'd say, 'OK, just don't let it happen again.' Now, Coach Beamer said we're going to have to run every time we're late. And we want that. It's what we need."

Our next game was Nov. 14 against No. 3 Miami. We were 37-point underdogs, but with five minutes to go, the score was tied, and their fullback, Melvin Bratton fumbled into the end zone

We recovered.

But one of the officials had inadvertently blown his whistle before the play, and another official ruled that one of our tackles had lined up offside. If an inadvertent whistle hadn't cost us that turnover, they would have had to carry me out of the Orange Bowl on a stretcher. But our guy never should have lined up offside.

The next play, Bratton banged it in for a score. We ended up losing, 27-13, but after the game, defensive lineman Greg Drew said, "We took things more seriously in practice this week," he said. "We didn't let the little things slide."

I saw Miami coach Jimmy Johnson at the coaches'convention a few months later, and his first words to me were, "We were so lucky in that one. Your team almost cost us the national championship."

That game kind of shows you how important discipline is to a football game.

We won our last game that season, beating Cincinnati, 21-20, in frigid Lane Stadium before a crowd of 10,600. It was about 25 degrees, with a 25 mile-per-hour wind, and the students were home on Thanksgiving break.

"When we get this program back to where it should be, the people I'm going to appreciate are the 10,000 who were out there today," I said after the game. "They've got a little something to 'em, too."

I still have a fond place in my heart for those fans. One day, I'd like to have a get-together for those people and treat them to dinner. However, if I did that, I guess 80,000 would probably show up!

After the first year I had to find a replacement for my defensive coordinator, Ron Zook, who went to Ohio State. Ron was from Ohio, and Ohio State was a place where he had always dreamed of coaching. Ron and I had been through some difficult times that season. When it was over, it wasn't as rosey as when we started.

I remember being in a defensive meeting after the South Carolina game in 1987. They had beaten us 40-10 — our worst loss since 1982. The Gamecocks quarterback, sophomore Todd Ellis had passed for 334 yards without an interception. They had 502 yards of total offense.

"I really think we're getting away from the basics of our defense," I said.

Ron looked at me and said, "Then why did you hire me to be your defensive coordinator?"

You have to understand the stress we were under. We'd go into the office at 7 a.m. and stay till 2 a.m. We had graduate assistants sleeping on couches.

That night, Me, Billy Hite, Larry Creekmore and Ron were sitting sit in the meeting chain-smoking. The rest of my staff was probably miserable in there.

So when Ron said that, I lost it. I kicked the chalk tray and chalk and erasers went flying. I could sort of see the rest of my staff cringing. They had probably wondered what kind of deal they had gotten into here.

I can't blame him for leaving. We're still good friends. Now he's defensive coordinator for the New Orleans Saints. We talk quite a bit. I always understood why he left for Ohio State.

That winter, we had to save three scholarships for key returning personnel, and signed 14 players. It was my second recruiting class at Virginia Tech. After the NCAA sanctions were handed down, I said we couldn't afford to make any mistakes in recruiting, and looking back on that class, I thought we did pretty well:

Fullback Phil Bryant
Defensive end Don Davis
Defensive tackle Stephan Holloway
Offensive lineman Chris Holt
Tailback Tony Kennedy
Cornerback Greg Lassiter
Wide receiver Marcus Mickel

Defensive end Wooster Pack
Offensive lineman Skip Pavlik
Fullback Mark Poindexter
Free safety Damien Russell
Offensive lineman Marc Verniel
Defensive end David Wimmer
Quarterback Tommy Zban

That was a heck of a class. I'd take that class right now and go again. You liked to have a couple more linemen, but that's a pretty interesting class. Just about everybody played. And the guy who probably played the least, Zban, is a doctor now.

And the thing was, we were still developing our relationships with the state high schools. Maybe we were a little bit naive. Maybe the high school coaches around the state were thinking, "that new staff at Virginia Tech stinks." But I'm out there thinking, "We're Virginia Tech. Why wouldn't anybody not welcome us to their school?"

Now, we didn't exactly beat a lot of big schools for those players. It wasn't like we were going out and recruiting against the kind of people we're recruiting now. But those kids ended up being pretty good players.

That second year, 1988, we went 3-8, and I tried to be realistic. The reality of the situation is that we were kind of an average team going through a transition with a redshirt freshman quarterback, Will Furrer.

And we were playing the toughest schedule in the country, according to the NCAA. We weren't getting blown out every week; we were competitive. The kids were playing pretty good. There were positive things to draw from. We just wanted to hang around long enough to get enough wins. But that schedule was something. Our very first game, we had to go to Death Valley to face No. 4 Clemson, when the Tigers had Terry Allen. There was a crowd of 80,500 in there that day.

The Tigers have a tradition at Death Valley. Before they get introduced, they stand at the top of a hill in the end zone, next to "Howard's Rock," a tribute to their coaching legend, Frank Howard.

Two years earlier, in 1986, the Tigers were standing up there and some of the Hokie players beckoned at them to "come on down." It was the Tech players' way of saying they weren't intimidated. It must have worked because they beat Clemson that day, 20-14.

I thought our kids might try something like that again, but I was hoping against it. I mean, Clemson already remembered what happened in 1986. We didn't need to upset that crowd any more than we had to. But I didn't want our kids to back down from them, either.

So we go out on the field and, sure enough, there are my guys jumping out on the field, challenging the Tigers to come down that hill.

And then I looked again, and upon further review, I realized it was all my second team guys, not the ones who were getting ready to go into battle. There was not one first-teamer out there.

"Aw geez, great," I'm thinking. "Just what we need. Let's get them all riled up." We lost, 40-7.

It was kind of like that all season. We'd watch the film of Syracuse, and go, "aw, geez. These guys are good." We'd coach like heck all week, but it was so uphill. The chances of winning were so small; everything would have to go right.

Then it would be Sunday night again, and we'd start looking at film of No. 7 West Virginia. And we'd go, "aw, geez."

Then it would be No. 8 South Carolina. "Aw, geez."

And later it would be No. 5 Florida State. "Aw, geez."

We'd see film of these teams and we just knew we were outmanned. I'd look around the room at my staff and could tell they were thinking, "just how the heck are we going to beat all of these great teams?"

And on it went. That schedule included four Top 10 teams and six Top 20 teams. WVU went 11-0 and played Notre Dame in the Fiesta Bowl; Florida State went 10-1 and played Auburn in the Sugar Bowl; Clemson went 9-2 and played Oklahoma in the Citrus Bowl; Syracuse went 9-2 and played LSU in the Hall of Fame Bowl.

Southern Miss had Brett Favre, finished 9-2 and went to the Independence Bowl. South Carolina went 8-3 and went to the Liberty Bowl. And Louisville and Virginia finished with winning records.

We just kept waiting for an opponent where you think, "alright! Here we go! This is one we can win!" And it never came.

Vaughn Hebron turned out to be the jewel of 1989 recruiting class, but the biggest player was the one who got away.

We were in the running for linebacker Robert Jones, who went on play for the Dallas Cowboys and now plays for the Miami Dolphins. He was from Nottoway, Va., an area we had been strong in for years. He was good friends with Lawrence White, a great linebacker for us who has since passed away.

Robert committed to us verbally out of high school, but did not qualify academically. He enrolled at Fork Union, where he continued to improve his test scores. Until he did, we could not guarantee his acceptance.

It was late January when Robert's scores came in, and he had passed. I was so relieved. I called him to congratulate him and welcome him to Blacksburg.

"Coach, I'm going to East Carolina," he said.

This came as a shock to me. I had to ask him why.

"I want to reward their loyalty," he said.

While Robert was at Fork Union, it turned out that East Carolina had told him, "Why are you sweating it? Come on over here. We can guarantee your admission."

That was tough to accept, but I respected his decision.

We just had to go through a period of time where we had to earn some confidence with the admissions department. There were scars from the previous situation that were so strong, that they weren't going to just change overnight.

In the meantime we were just trying to tread water.

11

A KNOCKOUT SEASON

THE 1989 SEASON was one of good things, bad things and ugly things.

The good: We had our first winning season, going 6-4-1, including an upset of No. 9 West Virginia in Morgantown.

The bad: Cheryl's father died shortly after that game. So did my high school coach, Tommy Thompson.

More bad: I suffered chest pains at East Carolina and missed the Tulane game after an angioplasty.

The ugly: A brawl ended our game at Virginia, and I lost my right front tooth.

Once again, we suffered severe personnel losses to start the year. This time we were without most valuable player Horacio Moronta, starting safety Scott Rice and starting tailback Ralph Brown because of academics. And top recruit James Wilson was not admitted because he did not meet our university's stricter-than-the NCAA-required entrance standards.

But we beat Akron in our opener, Tech's first season-opening win since 1984. We started the season 2-1-1 and next up was West Virginia and Major Harris. We were 16-point underdogs.

After we arrived in Morgantown my son, Shane, found a copy of the WVU student newspaper, and in it they referred to Virginia Tech as "a second-class program." Well, after that, I got all of our players together at the Holiday Inn for our Friday night meeting. I then held up that paper.

"There's an article in this paper that says Virginia Tech is a second-class program," I said. "Well, I'm from Hillsville and we didn't have very much growing up, but nobody ever called us second class."

I could tell our players related to that. Our strength coach, Mike Gentry, told me that was when he knew this was finally MY football team — not Bill Dooley's team.

"The players could tell you were speaking from the heart," Gentry later said. "They made the connection. When I left that meeting, I knew we were going to win that game."

We shut down Major Harris, Mickey Thomas kicked four field goals and we upset the Mountaineers, 12-10. Some of our players danced on the field after that game, and I know it really upset some of West Virginia's fans.

"This is a new day for Virginia Tech football," I told a large group of supporters who greeted us at the airport upon our return.

They say bad things happen in threes. That Wednesday, Cheryl's father died, which was devastating. Then we lost to Florida State, 41-7 in Blacksburg, when Peter Tom Willis had a big day against us. Then we went down to Greenville to play East Carolina on Oct. 21 and lost, 14-10.

I was OK in the first half of the game, but in the third quarter,

I felt this painful tightness. John Ballein looked at me and said I was white as a ghost. I knew something was wrong. I then went over to see our team doctor, Duane Lagan, who was on the sidelines.

"I need you to check me out as soon as this game is over," I said.

I never thought it was something as serious as a heart attack, but I knew something was not right.

The tightness had gone away, but Dr. Lagan was on top of it enough to be concerned, and recommended I go to the hospital for some tests. I went to Blacksburg Hospital on Sunday. On Monday, they sent me to Roanoke Memorial Hospital and kept me there.

On Tuesday Billy Hite pinch-hit for me at the weekly press conference at the Red Lion Inn.

"We know he's going crazy not being here with us," Billy said, "but he's keeping in touch. He keeps telling me to make sure his favorite play, 62-Racer, is in the game plan."

The next day was Wednesday, Oct. 25th; I underwent a transluminal coronary angioplasty to relieve what was believed to be 90-95% blockage of an artery leading to my heart. I wasn't nervous until the catheterization before the operation. When I saw that one of the arteries to my heart was almost cut off, I got a little scared.

They inserted a tiny balloon into one of my arteries via a guide catheter and inflated it until the cholesterol plaque causing the blockage was pushed back. I was awake for the procedure. To be honest, when I was getting it done, it kinda felt like the tightness I had experienced Saturday, because they're blowing that balloon up in there to get things unclogged. It was a little scary, but it only lasted 8-10 seconds.

After the procedure, we had a press conference at the hospital, and one of the reporters asked me if stress contributed to my heart problem.

"I'll tell you what stress is," I told him. "Stress is laying on the operating table and suddenly realizing that three of the four doctors around you are West Virginia graduates."

I had visions of our players dancing on their field, and how mad their fans got, and I'm thinking, "aw, geez. My life is in the hands of three Mountaineers!"

The lead doctor, Dr. Robert Rude, was great. He told me there had been no heart attack at East Carolina and that the chest pains were a warning sign.

"You're very lucky," he said. "If this went untreated, it is likely you would have experienced a heart attack or further angina. Now, with some minor lifestyle changes, there is a very low chance of that occurring."

I quit smoking cigarettes after that. I had smoked kind of off and on for I don't know how many years. The funny thing was, I had quit that previous summer but had started up again.

It began when we were vacationing in Charleston, S.C., and in the middle of the week I had gone to Northern Virginia to speak at a Hokie Club function.

Cheryl took me to the airport and they had construction, changing the road pattern. We got lost and I was running late for my flight. We finally got there with about three minutes to spare. I ran to catch my plane, and I was stressed out, and Hokie Club fund-raiser John Moody was there in DC to pick me up.

I got in his car and smelled cigarette smoke. John was an old smoking buddy of mine, and he lit one up. I hadn't had a cigarette in about two months, but I felt like I really needed one. "I think I'll smoke just one, just to relax," I said, and asked him for one. About 10 minutes later, I said, "John, I think I'll smoke two."

That's how I started back. And after the season started I was smoking a lot.

But after that angioplasty, I gave it up for good and haven't smoked a cigarette since.

I had to miss our next game, at home against Tulane. Billy Hite took over the head coaching duties.

"Billy has moved all of his things into your office," said one of our administrators, Sharon McCloskey. She was joking, but he did steal the cigarettes out of my desk. He figured I didn't need them anymore.

Friday night Billy took the team to the regular Friday night movie. The seniors picked "Shocker." Billy said it was the worst movie he had ever seen. So maybe being in the hospital wasn't all bad.

Saturday morning, I just had to get out of there. I went up to Lane Stadium. The doctors didn't want me to do it, but gave me permission. Billy tried to get me in the locker room to say something to the kids, but the doctors just wouldn't allow me to do that. As I went to leave, our quarterback Will Furrer saw me.

Will and I had an interesting relationship. We could disagree on things, but there was always this bond. And when he came out there, we hugged, and I just lost it, and he just lost it. We didn't say anything. We were both just bawling.

Billy did a great job that day, and we beat Tulane, 30-13. I sat in my living room and watched it from home, and to be honest, I got to worrying a little bit that they didn't really need me.

I came back that next week and we beat Vanderbilt, 18-0, on Nov. 4th. Then came our big showdown at Virginia on Nov. 11th.

It was a hard-fought game, and we had our chances, but with time running out Virginia led, 32-25, and had the ball. They were just running out the clock.

One of our defensive ends, Jimmy Whitten, just couldn't stand Virginia. The quarterback was kneeling down, and usually when you do that, everybody just kind of stands there. But

Virginia's linemen were diving at our guy's knees. That's all Jimmy needed to get him going.

He and one of their offensive linemen exchanged words. The same thing happened after the second snap. I saw a problem coming.

The final whistle blew, students began running out on the field and I was afraid a brawl was going to start.

I then ran out there to try to stop Jimmy from hitting this guy, but by the time I got there Jimmy had drawn back his arm. His elbow hit me in the mouth — just nailed me — and knocked out my right front tooth.

The tooth had gotten damaged a little during a high school basketball game. I think the root was weak, and it had turned a little bit brown; it was a little bit different from the other teeth. But when Jimmy hit it just right, that tooth popped right out.

I fell to my knees in the middle of the field, a riot going on around me, and Cheryl was in the stands thinking I'm having a heart attack.

Jimmy turns around and said, "oh my gosh!" I told him I was OK, except for my tooth.

At that point, he got down on the ground with me, looking for the tooth, with people running all around us. I was thinking at the time: "This is a helluva thing. We just got our butts kicked, people are swarming all around me, I'm on my hands and knees looking for my tooth. How much worse can this get?"

I found out later my wife was up in the stands, thinking I was dying.

I mean I looked awful after the game. And I still had to do the postgame press conference, but I was having problems because I couldn't say my "F's."

The team doctors cleaned the area that had been bleeding and I think our team dentist, Dr. Stanton, finally found the tooth. He tried gluing it back in, so it wouldn't look so bad, but the tooth couldn't be replaced. A few days later he made me a bridge. So at least now my smile is a little brighter.

The next week, we beat North Carolina State, 25-23, in Raleigh, giving us our first winning season at Virginia Tech.

12

IT'S GOTTA BE
THE SHOES

IT WAS A NEW decade, the nineties. We were coming off a 6-4-1 season and got some big recruits. Things were looking up.

We brought in center Jim Pyne, quarterback Maurice DeShazo, cornerback Tyronne Drakeford, wide receiver Antonio Freeman and linebacker Ken Brown. Pyne and DeShazo were big ones for us, now. Those two were the ones the big schools really wanted, and we signed them. It helped us turn the corner.

Pyne was our first national recruit. A lot of big schools were after him: Michigan, Michigan State, Stanford, Clemson. He was a great player — he bench-pressed 430 pounds in high school — but he was also strong academically, which made him a super-attractive prospect.

"We can turn this thing around," I told Jim. "You can make a difference in our program."

Pyne's brother, George IV, was Brown's 1988 team captain, and two coaches on our staff, Denie Marie and Tommy Groom, both coached him at Brown. Denie really followed the thing out. Although he was just a volunteer coach, he was really responsible for Jim Pyne coming to Virginia Tech. I remember talking to Denie, trying to feel him out on Pyne early in the process.

"This guy is looking at schools like Michigan. Do you think we're wasting our time here?" I asked.

"Oh, no, no," Denie said. "I think we should hang in there and keep after him."

I flew up to Boston's Logan Airport to visit Jim and his family. I was a country boy in the big city, and what should have been a 45-minute trip became an hour and 45 minutes. They were really sympathetic toward me when I finally arrived and fed me a great meal. We really hit it off.

I felt good about our chances with Jim after he took his official visit. I always invite our recruits' parents over to my house. George Pyne and I sat in my living room and talked a long time, longer than I usually did with recruits' parents. I could tell he felt comfortable with me.

As for Maurice, I knew we were going to get him when he went to Virginia for his official visit, and on his way back home he drove up to Blacksburg to see some people here.

DeShazo was a big signee for us, because we finally beat Virginia head-on for a guy rated among the top five prospects in the state.

So we're all excited about the 1990 season, and what happened? First game, at Maryland, starting cornerback John Granby broke his jaw. At least we had guys like offensive guard Glenn Watts, tailback Ralph Brown and defensive back Scott Rice back in the program after sitting out a year.

That 1990 schedule ranked seventh-toughest in the nation. We finished 6-5 but we were competitive in every game.

I already talked about our game with Florida State that year. We nearly beat them. We almost beat Georgia Tech, the year Bobby Ross won the national championship (along with Colorado).

But there was one game we lost that we never should have lost. We had faced FSU and West Virginia in consecutive weeks and went up to play Temple. The Owls had also beaten Wisconsin that year, so they weren't bad.

After the very first play of the game, I knew we were in trouble. There was no intensity. "Aw, geez," I said. "We're not ready to play."

And when you're not ready to play, that's when guys get hurt. Plus, that artificial turf in Veteran's Stadium was terrible. There were uneven places where the crew had covered up the baseball pitching mound and base areas, and it was like carpet on top of plywood.

Temple linebacker Santo Stephens hit our quarterback, Will Furrer, out of bounds, knocking him out of the game. Guys were falling like flies. By the fourth quarter, we were missing Furrer, Pyne, taiback Vaughn Hebron and safety Damien Russell. All four of those guys later played in the NFL.

We lost, 31-28. Walking off that field in Philadelphia, that was the sickest I felt all year.

We had Southern Mississippi in Blacksburg next, and man, we really needed to win. I really don't think our fans realized how good Southern Miss was that year. They had Brett Favre at quarterback, but the thing that impressed me most was how big they were.

I remember standing on the sideline before the game, watching them warm up and going, "oooh, geeez." That was the most nervous I felt all season.

But we won, 20-16. Furrer outplayed Favre, completing 24

of 34 passes for 247 yards and a touchdown. Favre was 16 of 30 for 192 yards, one touchdown and two interceptions.

The next week, we beat North Carolina State by the same score, 20-16.

We were 5-4 and still in bowl consideration when we flew down to Atlanta to play No. 7 Georgia Tech on Nov. 10. The Peach, All-American and Liberty bowls were looking at us. We really needed to pull that upset, but it was a tough game for me because I was facing my good friend, Bobby Ross.

I didn't enjoy that experience. We needed to win so bad, and there was a guy I really respect on the other side, and he's got a team vying for the national championship.

We played without our top two tailbacks, Hebron and Brown, but we took a 3-0 lead and held that till late in the fourth quarter. Then Scott Sisson kicked two field goals in the last 5:09, the game winner coming with eight seconds left, and we lost, 6-3.

The key play came when Georgia Tech receiver William Bell looked like he was juggling the ball out of bounds at the our 41. The officials ruled it a catch. The play set up the winning field goal.

At 5-5, we had no real shot at a bowl game. It was frustrating because we were so close. We were playing all these top-ranked teams, and lost four times after leading or holding a tie going into the final period.

But we had one game left: at home against Virginia. That was our bowl game. It was the big state showdown and the mood was electric. I think it was the greatest I had ever seen Lane Stadium until the 1999 season.

Our seniors got the idea that they wanted to wear all-maroon outfits with black shoes. One of our seniors, linebacker Archie Hopkins, said it gave us a meaner image. The maroon pants were OK with me, but I didn't know anything about those black shoes.

I then went downstairs, and the kids are all outside with these cans of black spray paint. Our equipment manager, Lester Karlin, is kind of a small guy, but you don't want to cross him. Well, he was having a fit, cussing and yelling, and I asked him what was wrong. He pointed over there, and when I saw what those guys were doing I'm not sure I wasn't having a few words, too.

I went up to Billy Hite and said, "our kids are worried way too much about their shoes."

Billy had a pretty good idea of what was going on, though. "I think we ought to kind of let them go where they're going," he said.

I invited Coach Claiborne in town for the game and took him to our pregame dinner. The students were gone for Thanksgiving break so we had our meal on campus, and our kids were kinda loud. When I played under Coach Claiborne, you didn't say a word at the pregame meal. He couldn't believe how loose our kids were, and how loose I was. I told him I felt really good about this game.

Then our kids walked across the street to our locker room and put on those outfits. It was the first time we had worn all-maroon outfits since 1984, and the first time we had worn black shoes since 1977.

Let me tell you, we looked ugly. I walked up to John Ballein before the game and told him so.

"I tell you what," I said. "We're either going to embarrass ourselves, or we're going to play great."

We played great. That was a magical night. It was our first-ever ESPN telecast. My old friend and boss at Murray State, Mike Gottfried, was in the booth with Sean McDonough. Kevin Kiley was working the sidelines. It was a 4:08 start, and everyone had been tailgating all afternoon. The lights were on, the stands were packed with 54,157 fans — the largest crowd ever to see a football game in Virginia at the time. It was the loudest I'd ever heard a crowd in Lane Stadium.

I was here in 1966 when we played Florida State, and I never remember the place being that loud. But that night I could actually hear the crowd over my headset.

Virginia was good, too. The Cavaliers were ranked No. 17 and had been ranked No. 1 earlier in the season and already had a Sugar Bowl bid locked up. It helped us that their quarterback, Shawn Moore, was out with a thumb injury, and they went with Matt Blundin.

We went out and won, 38-13. Fans rushed the field and the goalposts came down. It was really something.

We've worn black shoes ever since.

It might have been only for four hours, but it was a time we had the national television cameras in Blacksburg, a ticket couldn't be found and the whole university community had a feeling of togetherness — the students, faculty, alumni and townspeople. When I came here that's what I had dreamed about. Not many things on this campus can do that.

That game was so big from a recruiting aspect, too. It gave us a chance to show Virginia Tech in a positive light to a lot of people. Clemson has recruited so well for so long and a major part of their recruiting is that atmosphere on game day. Their recruits on the field with that big place packed and rocking.

We finished the year 6-5. We had our first back-to-back winning seasons against top-flight competition. Exactly half of our opponents earned bowl bids and 15 of the 22 teams we played had winning records, including seven teams ranked in the Top 25.

Things were finally turning around for us. Then, on Thursday, Dec. 13, 1990, we got even better news. Mike Tranghese announced that the Big East would add football to its conference structure beginning with the 1991 season, and Tech would be among four non-Big East schools (Temple, Rutgers, West Virginia) joining Syracuse, Pittsburgh and

My parents,
Herma and
Raymond
Beamer, at the
1995 Sugar
Bowl.

My brother and sisters with me in front of my grandmother's
house in Fancy Gap (left to right) Betty, Billie Jean and Barnett.
I'm the distracted one in the front right.

I played quarterback at Hillsville High. I was lucky enough to make All-State and All-Southern and throw for **43 TD's**.

Our basketball team at Hillsville posted a 12-6 record in 1964-65. I wore jersey #42, played guard and probably shot too much.

At Tech, I got moved from quarterback to defensive back on my second day. I later became a starter and a team captain in 1968.

Playing defensive back at Tech was not a high-profile postion, but it did allow me (25) the opportunity to steal a few passes.

The Radford coaching staff in 1969: (left to right) Ronald Lindon, head coach Harold Absher and me.

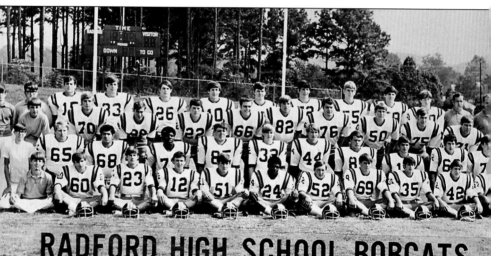

Our 1971 Radford High team won the 2-A state championship. I'm on the far right standing next to Norm Lineburg.

Jerry Clairborne's grad assistants at Maryland in 1972: (left to right) Thomas Park (kneeling), Brett Hart, Ralph Friedgen, Charles Rizzo and me.

Bobby Ross (middle) asked me to join his staff at The Citadel in 1974. I'm on the far right.

I joined Mike Gottfried's staff at Murray State in 1979 as the defensive coordinator. Mike's the one in the front row with all of the hair.

After Mike Gottfried left to go to Cincinnati after the 1980 season, I got the head-coaching job. This is my first staff in 1981.

The Beamer gang in Murray, Ky., in 1983. (left to right) Cheryl, Casey, me and Shane.

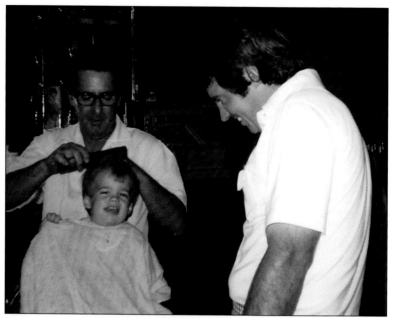

Shane didn't like his first hair cut at the local barber shop.

All-Pro defensive lineman Randy White of the Dallas Cowboys (right) helped us during a football camp at Murray State one year. I was a graduate assistant when Randy was at Maryland.

My college coach, Jerry Claiborne (left), has been my mentor and friend. He later coached at Maryland and Kentucky.

After we tied for the OVC championship in 1986, Casey got lost in the celebration. When Cheryl and I found her at midfield, it was a happy reunion.

Meeting the press in Blacksburg in December 1986 after accepting the head-coaching job at Virginia Tech.

My 1988 staff at Tech. We struggled to a 3-8-0 record that season.

Cheryl and Shane congratulated me after our first win at Tech in 1987 — a 31-11 romp over Navy in Blacksburg.

I was invited to coach the East team at the 1998 East-West Shrine Game in San Francisco.

Governor George Allen honored Cheryl and I at the Virginia State Assembly after Tech defeated Texas in the 1995 Sugar Bowl.

Texas coach John Mackovic and I were amazed about the size and weight of the Sugar Bowl trophy.

I was lucky to visit with two greats during a trip to Seattle in 1998: Tech grad and Texas Rangers manager Johnny Oates (right) and Seattle Mariners manager Lou Pinnella (left) whose son, Derek, played at Tech.

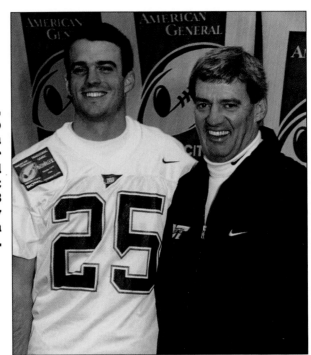

My son, Shane, who snapped on punts for Tech, posed with me at the 1998 Music City Bowl in Nashville.

Visiting with coaching friends (left to right) Joe Paterno of Penn State, R.C. Slocumb of Texas A&M, and Larry Smith and his wife, Cheryl, of Missouri, on a recent Nike trip.

Freshman quarterback Michael Vick (right) finished third in the 1999 Heisman voting.

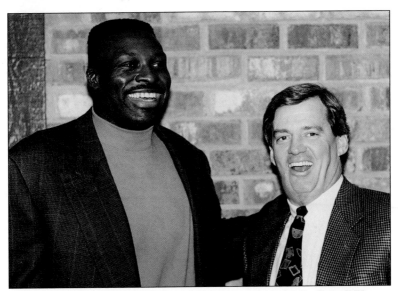

Bruce Smith (left), the All-Pro defensive end of the Buffalo Bills and now with the Washington Redskins, is one of Tech's many great players in the NFL.

President Bill Clinton called the locker room to congratulate Tech on its hard-fought showing against Florida State in the 2000 Sugar Bowl.

The Beamer gang posed with former President George Bush at the Bear Bryant Coach of the Year Award dinner in Houston.

brand-new additions, Miami and Boston College.

We had gotten a taste of the big-time with the ESPN win over Virginia, and now we had the biggest factor our program had been missing: conference affiliation. It gave us a recruiting edge we had never had before. It gave us a chance to put our young men on all-conference teams. It gave us a chance for a league championship. Our program's potential was greater than at any time in its history.

So it's kind of ironic that, the next day, I visited Boston College.

BC officials had offered me a six-year, $160,000-a-year deal. I was making $103,000 at Tech, but I really wasn't looking for a pay raise. There was a budgetary freeze on all state employees' raises, and I didn't feel comfortable about getting a raise unless everyone else was getting them. Money has never been a driving force for me in any decision I've ever made.

But at my age in the coaching business, you look at opportunities to be successful. You look at opportunities for security. By looking into the Boston College job, it was no slight at Virginia Tech.

I looked seriously at the job. I was tremendously impressed with the people there. The program had great promise, too. They had enjoyed great seasons in the past and potential for great seasons in the future. There were people on my staff who were convinced I was going to take it. But I'll tell you why I didn't. It was a couple of reasons.

A funny thing happened as I was getting ready to catch the plane for Boston. Will Furrer was at the Roanoke airport, catching a plane to Washington. The two of us started in this together and had been through some tough times. We shared that cry after my heart problem. If I was looking for some kind of sign, maybe that was one.

Cheryl and I flew on to Boston, and on Sunday we were looking at housing. Most of the assistants couldn't afford a nice house near the city, so they all lived about an hour away. I got to thinking about that. At Tech, we all lived within a 15-minute drive. If we worked late, it wasn't a big deal, because you could get right home.

But at Boston College, the coaches had that long commute. And then I remembered all the trouble I had on that recruiting trip to see Jim Pyne, and got to thinking how I might not be a city guy.

Cheryl and I talked on the plane on the way home. We reconfirmed our feelings that we wanted to be at Virginia Tech. We love this area. We had a lot of fan support. My family was secure here. And I felt good about this community. Shane was in the eighth grade and my daughter, Casey was in the fourth grade, and they had her friends. Cheryl and I liked the idea of rearing our kids in Blacksburg

I called Boston College athletic director Chet Gladchuk on Sunday night, Dec. 16th, and withdrew my name from consideration, then told Tech athletic director Dave Braine the next morning. I didn't want it to be a back and forth thing.

When all was said and done, the two most important things to me were my family and my players at Virginia Tech. This school gave me the opportunity to coach at this level. This was my alma mater and I felt a great sense of loyalty to the university. There was great potential to improve at Tech and I believed I could take the program to new heights.

Things were looking great for us. At the preseason media session in August 1991, I recalled the song *We've Only Just Begun* by the Carpenters. That's how I felt about our program. We had fought through personnel losses, the NCAA sanctions, tighter academic restrictions and an upgraded schedule.

Yet we were still here. Goods things were bound to be around the corner.

13

TURN UP
THE WICK

AT A POINT in the game, or in life, sometimes you have to turn up the intensity to get the best out of everyone. I call it "turning up the wick."

It usually makes the difference in winning and losing.

Another fact that makes the difference in winning and losing is paying attention to details.

And as a coach, you always want to make sure everybody knows what to do, and when to do it. You can assume nothing.

A great example was in 1990 and we were playing Southern Mississippi, who had Brett Favre at quarterback.

As a coach, you always want to make sure everybody knows what to do. You can assume nothing.

We led, 20-14, late in the game and were trying to run out the clock. Southern Miss had called its last timeout. We were on the far end of the field, and our quarterback, Will Furrer, came trotting over. Will was an English major with a 3.8 grade-point average. A very bright guy. We discussed what play to run, came to a decision and Will ran back out to the huddle.

Then I remembered something. "Will! Will! Will!" I screamed. "Come here! Come here! Come here!"

Will ran all the way back across the field over to me. I grabbed him by the jersey and pulled him close and looked him in the eye.

"Remember now, if we get this first down, the game's over!" I said.

Will looked straight at me.

"No shit," he said.

Will was a Fork Union kid. We've always had good success with quarterbacks from Fork Union: Furrer, Jim Druckenmiller, Al Clark. We think head coach John Shuman does a great job. We have a good relationship with him. It also helps that our junior varsity squad plays them every year. Fork Union usually wins, but the game gives us a chance to see their players up close.

We always let our graduate assistants coach our jayvees against Fork Union. It's good experience for them and gives them a break from the usual mundane things they have to do. These days, I just go out to the game to scout the Fork Union players. But back then I sometimes got involved in the game.

Well, one year, it might have been 1992 when we were really struggling; graduate assistant Steve Hale was the head jayvee coach.

Steve played at Tech from 1985-88 and was always one of my favorites. He was our deep snapper even though he only stood about 5-foot-7. But he was a sturdy little guy who was a heck of a snapper; he was the one who snapped the ball to Chris Kinzer during that great 1986 season when Tech won the Peach Bowl. But with his little short legs I was concerned about his coverage ability downfield.

It was just before halftime, and Fork Union was beating us again. They pinned us in deep with a punt and we had the ball on our own one-yard line. Hale said, "submarine it! Submarine it!" He just wanted to run a dive play, let the clock run out and regroup.

I was standing behind him. "No, no, no," I said. "We need to throw that pass, that quick pass in there. Let's attack. They won't be expecting it." It was a screen pass that had been working pretty well.

Steve shook his head; he didn't like the call. But we tried that quick pass and Fork Union sacked our quarterback, Tommy Zban, for a safety.

Steve threw off his headset and whirled around at me.

"Coach, how about from now on, you do your coaching on Saturday, and I'll do mine on Friday!"

The people standing around us couldn't believe it. They thought I was going to chew Steve out.

But he was right. It turned out to be a bad call, and he had the guts to tell me. There was no way I could chew him out.

I've never been a guy who gets mad when things are going bad. If anything, I get calmer. I'm more likely to lose it when things are going good. But there was one notable exception.

It was during halftime of the 1987 Tulane game. We were getting hammered. As we were heading to the locker room, assistant coach Tommy Groom told me, "Coach, you gotta get in there and go off on them."

"You're right," I said. "I'm gonna get after 'em."

For 15 out of the next 20 minutes I ranted and raved. I kicked chairs and pounded my fist. Sweat was flying off my forehead and my face got red.

And what happened? The opening kickoff of the second half went whoosh! Tulane returned it for a touchdown.

But make no mistake about it, I like to win. Whether it's

college football, racquetball, golf or video black jack, I want to win at everything I do.

A great example of how competitive my staff can be is our lunchtime racquetball games.

In a recent game this spring, it was me and John Ballein against Rickey Bustle and Bryan Stinespring. We were playing to seven, and Rickey hit a kill shot that would have made it 6-5. Rickey was getting ready to serve again.

"Oh, no, no, no," I said. "That shot skipped."

"No, that didn't skip," Rickey said.

"Play it over!" Bryan said, ever the diplomat.

Rickey looked at John. "Did it skip?" he said.

"No, coach," John said. "It was a good shot."

Man, I was mad. It was time to turn up the wick! Rickey served the ball and I swung at it as hard as I could. I hit the ball into the ground and they won. As we were walking out I slammed my fist into the door. It's amazing that I didn't break my hand.

Behind my back, I heard Bryan talking to John. "For the record," he whispered, "I said, 'play it over!'"

Golf, now, is a little more relaxing. I'll tell you why I like golf: the scenery of the course. I don't like phones out there. That's one of my requirements: you don't carry that cell phone out on the course with me.

But it's the toughest game I've ever tried to play. About the time you think you've got it, you start hitting sideways.

My philosophy in golf is, it doesn't matter how much money you win. It's that you win.

We have a regular golf foursome of me, my buddy Wayland Overstreet (Street), former WSLS sports anchor Greg Roberts and John Ballein. We put a little money in for fun, nothing big. It usually always amounts to a dollar or two. Well, early in the spring of 1999 they won our first match of the year, and Greg took a picture of us handing over our bets. He was going on about how every time they beat us, he was going to take a picture and hang it up in his bar in Roanoke. But they never beat us again.

During the summer of 1999 we went down to Myrtle Beach for a weekend and beat them, and I'm having fun, saying, "Where's the camera? Where's the camera?" I went out and bought a little disposable camera, and had a lady in the restaurant take a picture of John and Greg giving Street and me our dollar.

John and Greg had billed our last match of the year, as "The Match of the Millennium." It wasn't one we wanted to lose, because we'd hear about it all winter. Sure enough John and Greg beat us, and they were really crowing. Street paid John his money and Greg took their picture. I was over there sulking and saw John whisper to Greg, but I had no idea he had a camera. As I walked over to pay Greg his winning dollar, he pulled his camera out from behind his back and took a picture of our hands exchanging the dollar bill.

"The camera!" I said. "The camera!" And they got a big laugh over it. Only I wasn't laughing. "What I'M saying is, that camera doesn't have to BE out here," I said.

Another time Street and I were ahead going into the last hole. John and Greg wanted to go double or nothing. "Absolutely not," I said. "We fought over the original bet all the way through. Why would we change that on the eighteenth hole?" We worked it out so that if Street and me got beat on the hole, we would still win one dollar. The important thing to me wasn't how much money we won. It was that we won.

Street and I go way back. We were roommates when I was coaching at Radford. We lived in the basement of a two-level condo in Fairlawn. For a bed, I just had a box spring and mattress sitting on the cement floor. One night it rained really hard. I woke up in the morning and there was a puddle of water in the middle of my room. I heard this weird noise, and

I looked over there and saw a frog in the puddle, croaking.

I then went in Street's room and woke him up.

"Street," I said, "I think it's time to upgrade."

I like to relax on the golf course, but sometimes I can't help but doing a little coaching out there. One year I took my son, Shane, to golf school in Florida. The pro worked on Shane's swing, getting his hands and stance right. "I think I got it," Shane said. I wasn't so sure, so after the pro left, so I gave Shane a few more pointers. I saw him kind of shake his head. When I was done, he walked over to John Ballein.

"I know Dad is paying a lot for these lessons," he said to John, "but I didn't know he was paying for TWO people to teach me."

The third day at that golf school, it was hot, about 90 degrees. We had hit balls from 9 a.m. to noon, then played 18 holes. Old John was just dying from the heat. His shirt was soaked through with sweat and his face was sunburned. He was thirsty and I could tell all he wanted was to take a shower. But the coach in me knew he needed a little more work on his draw, so I took him back over to the range. I took my shaving kit out and put it in front of the tee box.

"John, take this five-iron and hit the ball just outside of my shaving kit," I said. This is a good drill that works, now. And if you swing properly, you won't hit my bag.

"Coach, I'm going to hit your bag," John said.

"No, what I'M saying is, hit the ball on the OUTSIDE of this bag," I said.

"I'm gonna hit it!" he said, but he knew there was no argu-ing with me. He reared back and knocked the living daylights out of my shaving kit.

"Oh no!" I remembered. "My glasses are in there!"

John tried to get away, but I said, "We're not done yet. Give me your flip-flop."

He took off his flip-flop and handed it to me. I set it down inside the ball and we stayed out there another 30 minutes until he got his swing right.

Another thing I really love is video black jack. They have those machines all over Myrtle Beach. Now, I can play some video black jack. I love it. It's fast. You don't have to wait for a dealer to re-shuffle. You just keep pushing buttons.

On that one trip with Street, Greg and John, that's what we did everyday: golf, dinner, play black jack.

That first day, Greg played four hands and was out. But I was doing pretty well, laughing, having a good time.

All week, everybody seemed to lose but me. Toward the end of the trip, we were riding in a limo. "I'll tell you what we need to do," I said. "There's a spot right up here that has one of those video black jack machines. I'm feeling lucky. Let's go in there, and each of us will put $20 down. What do you think about that?"

Greg says, "Coach, I'll tell you what. I'm just going to take my $20 and throw it out the window. Maybe some hobo will find it, so I won't feel like I'm just wasting my money."

My daughter, Casey, is really good at black jack. She knows when to split and when to double down.

We were at Hilton Head a couple of summers ago, in the bar area of a restaurant while we were waiting to be seated, and they had a black jack machine. She was too young to play so she looked over my shoulder, telling me what to do. Thanks to Casey we won $100, which paid for dinner.

Cheryl tells me, "When she gets married, she'll probably want to go to Las Vegas on her honeymoon instead of some romantic, tropical place."

I'll give you a quick lesson. It all gets into what the dealer has. People starting out get too caught up in their own cards. That's important, but half of the deal is what the dealer is showing. That's how you decide whether you hit or don't take a hit.

It's like John Engelberger said. "You've got to play the percentages." You always assume the dealer has a ten not showing, because there are more tens in the deck than anything else.

The ultimate is when the dealer is sitting with a six showing, and you've got eleven showing. You should double on that. You figure your chances are good the next card is going to be ten, giving you twenty-one, which can't be beat. Always double on eleven.

It's simple. I can't understand why Greg Roberts can't grasp it. I guess he's too busy talking.

The key is not to play too long. No way would I spend two or three hours playing that. You stay in there long enough, and that machine is going to get you.

14

ONE STEP UP, TWO STEPS BACK

ON FEB. 5, 1991, the Big East made it official. We were officially in, and I was happy.

Then I took a look at our schedule.

After our opener with James Madison, our next five games were away from Blacksburg. We needed a breakthrough season, and we had to face North Carolina State, South Carolina, Oklahoma, West Virginia and Florida State in a row on the road. And they were all good that year. When we played them, the Seminoles were No. 1; the Sooners were No. 6.

The FSU game was supposed to be our home game, but we moved it to the Citrus Bowl in Orlando, a "neutral" site. The Seminoles offered us a $800,000 guarantee, and our athletic department was strapped for money. A home game would have given us about $350,000 after expenses, so you're talking about an extra $450,000 in profits.

I think athletic director Dave Braine probably felt a little guilty about doing it. I'm sure he thought he was doing what he felt was right for the athletic department, because we needed the money.

Still, it was a tough thing for our football team. Remember, we had nearly beaten Florida State the year before. It wasn't like we had no chance to win the game.

The worst part came before kickoff. I was standing on the sidelines while Florida State was getting introduced. All their fans were in the stands doing the tomahawk chop, screaming and yelling, and out ran Marvin (Shade Tree) Jones.

"Aw, geez," I said.

Then out ran Terrell Buckley, who was high-stepping and high-fiving.

And these impressive players kept trotting out there and we're all thinking, "Aw, geez, look at the SIZE of these guys!"

Then I saw the worst thing of all.

Out came that damn Appaloosa horse.

"They're not supposed to have that damn horse here!" I was screaming. "This is OUR home game!"

We out-gained the Seminoles, 420-343, but had three interceptions and a fumble and lost, 33-20. After the game quarterback Will Furrer told our AD, "If that had been our crowd out there, we would have won the game." I think Dave believed him, because he later said, "Moving a home game for money, I would never do that to our kids again."

We lost four of those five games in that stretch, and every weekend was a gut-wrencher.

Our lone win came over West Virginia. We beat them, 20-14, in Morgantown with a little help from Mother Nature. The Mountaineers had just scored at the end of the third quarter when there was a flash of lightning. Officials delayed the game while the electrical storm passed. WVU really had the momentum, and the delay gave us a chance to get back in the locker room and regroup.

That was the only time I can ever remember a game being delayed because of the weather. And here's the crazy thing: while we were in the dressing room, the bands from both teams went running out on the field with their metal instruments.

The following week we went to Orlando for the FSU game, the last of our five-game road stretch. We arrived on Friday morning and our hotel rooms weren't ready. I turned to John Ballein and said, "Perfect, absolutely perfect."

We won our next three games before facing No. 14 East Carolina and quarterback Jeff Blake. Furrer's knee had locked up on him in pregame warmups, so we went with backup Rodd Wooten.

On our first drive of the second half we drove to the ECU 4-yard line. A touchdown would have given us a 21-7 lead. We sent in a "locked" play.

When a play is "locked," it means we run it, no matter what. There is no audible.

But Rodd saw something in ECU's alignment he didn't like and audibled to a pass, which ECU free safety Greg Grandison intercepted and raced 95 yards for a touchdown, tying the score. We lost, 24-17.

Next up was our season finale, with Virginia. In our Sunday staff meeting I told our offensive coaches, "we have to decide who we're going to go with at quarterback, Wooten or redshirt freshman Maurice DeShazo. When you're in your meetings this week, you decide."

So Thursday rolled around and I needed to know who was going to be our starting quarterback. I asked offensive coordinator Steve Marshall.

"I think we ought to go with DeShazo," he said.

I looked at quarterbacks coach Rickey Bustle. "I'm not about to change quarterbacks," he said. "I think we should stay with Wooten for now."

And I asked Tommy Groom and I asked Bryan Stinespring. They gave me their answers, and we were deadlocked. Half for DeShazo, and half for Wooten.

Then I looked at graduate assistant James (Bubba) Brown. His vote would break the tie.

"James, what do you think?"

"Coach," he drawled, "you ain't paying me enough to make THIS decision."

We ended up starting Wooten but also played DeShazo. It didn't matter. Virginia sacked us seven times and held us to a season-low 92 passing yards and hammered us, 38-0. It was a bitter end to a promising season. Instead of going to a bowl game, we finished 5-6.

In February, I let go of two of my original assistants at Tech, Duke Strager and Larry Creekmore.

That was very difficult. Both were good Hokies. They weren't bad coaches. But after a thorough evaluation of our staff, I felt we needed a fresh approach with new chemistry. We just needed to try something different.

I hired two Virginia Tech graduates, Terry Strock, Class of 1962, and George Foussekis, Class of '67, to replace them. Terry had been at Georgia Tech and George at Maryland. They were two guys who had many, many years of defensive experience.

When George had a change of heart and decided not to come aboard, there was never any doubt in my mind whom I would hire. It was going to be one of our graduate assistants, Todd Grantham, who played offensive line for me his senior year. I liked him all along. It was just a matter of him gaining experience. I knew he'd be a good coach if anybody would give him the chance.

Some people might have questioned the move. I mean, here I was giving an unproven graduate assistant a full-time job at a major Division I-A program. A lot of guys with more experience were out there looking for work. But there was never any question in my mind that he could do the job. I told Todd of his good fortune on March 12 at exactly 2:30 p.m.

Todd did a great job for us. So great, in fact, that Michigan State stole him from us after the 1995 season. Now he's coaching in the NFL for the Indianapolis Colts.

With my new staff in place, I looked ahead to the 1992 season with great expectations. Season ticket sales were around 12,000 — an all-time high at the time. Interest was rising. I was disappointed we had taken a step back in 1991, but we knew we were better than our record showed. It was time now to get the job done. It was time to turn up the wick.

Instead, I suffered through the worst year of my life.

Whatever the reason, we couldn't hold a lead in the fourth quarter. We led seven teams going into the final period and were down three points, six points and 12 points to three other teams in the fourth quarter. We had a legitimate shot to win 10 games that season, but finished 2-8-1, with our only Division I-A win against Temple — a school that went 1-10 and fired its coach.

It was one nightmare after another. We lost on the last play of the game at Rutgers. We were tied on the last play of the game against North Carolina State. And we blew an 11-point, fourth-quarter lead at Louisville. I mean, we had them beat. One of our defensive ends got frustrated and was flagged for a key 15-yard personal foul that really hurt us late in the game.

We choked that one away. "This was the toughest loss I've ever been associated with," I told the press afterward.

The Cardinals took a 21-17 lead with 3:07 to play.

Then with 30 seconds left, they were taking a knee. One of our defensive ends, Don Davis, couldn't take it anymore and stormed off the field. Defensive line coach Todd Grantham, a really fiery guy, was livid. He couldn't believe one of our players was heading back to the dressing room before the game was over. He ran after him, screaming. The two continued yelling at each other inside the locker room.

When the game was over, several other players got into dressing room arguments. Offensive lineman Damien McMahon was yelling at placekicker Ryan Williams. All hell was breaking loose and I didn't know it because I was still outside, answering reporter's questions. When I finally arrived in the dressing room everybody shut up. We were all frustrated, including me. What can you say after something like that? So I was up in front of the team and I said, "Does anybody have anything they'd like to say?"

I saw Billy Hite in the back of the room waving his arms back and forth as if to say, "No, coach! No!" But then Davis said, "yeah, I got something to say," and McMahon said, "yeah, me too," and all of sudden everybody was back at it again, screaming at each other.

Two games later we played defending national champion Miami. It was the first time a No. 1 team had ever visited Blacksburg, and we started a former walk-on quarterback, Treg Koel.

The week before the game Casey was laying in bed between me and Cheryl and we were watching the sports report on TV. The announcer came on and talked about how Miami of Ohio got beat, but Miami of Florida killed their opponent.

"Daddy," Casey said, "which Miami are we playing this week?"

"We're playing the Miami who killed their opponent," I said.

Casey frowned. "I wish we were playing the OTHER Miami," she said.

"I do, too," I said.

We lost, 43-23, and it wasn't that close. The Hurricanes led, 37-3, in third quarter and Dennis Erickson could have beaten us worse if he had wanted to.

As bad as those games were, the game at Rutgers on Halloween, Oct. 31, really summed up the season. We led, 28-7, at one point and 49-37 midway through the fourth quarter and we figured we had this one won.

But Rutgers cut the lead to 49-44 and forced us to punt. They took over at their own 22 with 1:32 left and no timeouts. Bryan Fortay, the Scarlet Knights' quarterback, completed three quick passes but we forced them into a third-and-seven situation from their own 39. We called timeout to set our defense.

Fortay then tried a deep Hail Mary pass to Mario Henry. Our linebacker was right on top of the play but was afraid of committing interference and Henry caught the ball for a 46-yard gain to our 15.

That's how that season went; it would've been better if he had committed interference, just a 15-yard penalty. Rutgers spiked the ball with five seconds left, then Fortay hit Chris Brantley with a 15-yard pass in the corner of the end zone and we lost, 50-49.

We had 558 yards of total offense, forced seven turnovers and scored 49 points. And lost.

That was the worst-coached game of my life.

Usually after each game I meet with the media and give a few brief comments then answer questions, but this time I had nothing to say. I just waited for them to ask the first question.

I knew our players were frustrated. "I can't believe some of these schools have beaten us," center Jim Pyne said following the Rutgers loss.

All that losing got into my mind, too. It was all I could think about. I couldn't sleep. The doctors prescribed some medication to help me sleep, but it made me feel all nervous and jittery, so I got off that stuff. It was a terrible year. We thought we were starting to turn things around. But instead, everything came crashing down.

Cheryl really helped me get through those tough times. She might not understand football exactly, but she understands when I'm hurting and when I need attention. She always wants to do something a little special; get a little gift that might mean something. She's always thinking of other people. When things were going bad for me, she was always trying to do her best to take some of the hurt away. She's been the perfect wife. She's there for me to talk to. She always is there to make me feel better.

As the losses mounted, I started getting threatening phone calls at home. The night we lost to Louisville, Casey, who was then 12, answered the phone. It was an irate fan who cursed me and told her how her father was such a lousy coach. When I came home she was sitting on the living room couch, crying.

I knelt down and asked her why she was crying. She told me about the phone call with the rude man.

"Casey, sometimes in life, you're up here," I said, and raised my hand toward the ceiling. "And sometimes you're down here," and I lowered my hand toward the floor. "Right now, we're down here, but don't you worry. Your daddy's a good coach. And we're going to be up here again."

It had never dawned on me that a certain percentage of alumni wanted me fired. I was too focused on trying to fix the problem.

After the season, I spoke at a Hokie Club function in Wytheville, Va. I went through the buffet line and sat down at the table with a group of alumni. My host turned to me and said, "Coach, I want you to meet John Beamer."

"John Beamer," I said. "We have the same last name. You know, I grew up right over that mountain, in Hillsville. We could be related."

He said, "Not this year, we're not."

The next season, after we won the 1993 Independence Bowl, I was invited to speak to the Wytheville Rotary Club. And the first guy I saw coming through the door was this John Beamer. He saw me and do you know what he said?

"Hello, cousin Frank!"

15

THE MOST
IMPORTANT HIRE
I EVER MADE

I WAS IN THE sixth year of my contract, and when you have a season like that where you only win two games, well, how many coaches survive that? The thought these days is, "Let's fire him and get someone else in here." It's amazing. I might be one of a kind.

Thank goodness for athletic director Dave Braine and school president Jim McComas and university administrator Minnis Ridenour. They believed in me. I think they saw that a good foundation for our program was in place. Although we weren't OK, I think they realized we were really close to being OK.

But we needed to make some difficult decisions.

Every Sunday morning around 7:30 or 8 during the season, Dave Braine came down to the football office with a big bag of fresh Carol Lee doughnuts. He sat in there with us in the film room and watched tape of the game and sometimes asked questions. "Why did you do this? Why did you do that?" I'd tell him why, and he usually seemed satisfied with the answers.

Later that day we would always meet privately and talk about the game.

When the losses mounted, Dave was honest with me. "You're not the problem," he said. "You're the right guy. You're doing the right things.

"But I don't think you can survive public opinion with the current coaching staff." But he never said, "You need to fire so and so."

I knew something needed to happen. We needed to change our course.

After the season I met with Dave again, on Monday, Nov. 23rd. Two days later, I dismissed assistant coach Tommy Groom, a good Hokie who had been with me from the beginning. I also reassigned defensive coordinator Mike Clark and defensive backs coach Keith Jones.

I had tried to make our coaching staff a family affair, but this is a business. When things are not successful, sometimes you have to make very tough, cruel decisions. In the end, you have to do what you can to make the situation better. It was no reflection on Tommy; I love the guy. I just wanted to make this whole thing fit together.

Then I scrapped our terminology of the wide-tackle six (also called an eight-man front) in favor of what we called a 4-3-4 alignment. The wide-tackle six defense had worked well for us through the years, both at Murray and Virginia Tech, but I just thought people needed to hear something different.

It's funny; we used that defense for years, but many people never understood why it was called the "wide-tackle six." Well, when this defense first started out under Alabama coach Bear Bryant, the defensive ends were called "tackles" and the tackles were called "guards," which tells you how long this defense has been around. At Tech, we really should have called it the "wide-END six."

What we play now is still a version of the wide-tackle six. It's a proven defense, and you see a lot of pro football teams using it today, sneaking that strong safety or the weak side cornerback or free safety up there a little closer to the line.

The idea of the wide-tackle six was simple: you wanted to get enough people up on the line to stop the run and make the other team throw the ball. You've heard that old expression: "Only three things can happen when you throw the ball, and two of them are bad." The wide-tackle six put the other team in a situation where they had to pass, and you'd know it was coming, so the odds of the two bad things — an incompletion or an interception — increased.

My first year at Tech, however, we found ourselves trying to find new ways to improve our defense. Defensive coordinator Ron Zook and I used to sit back in the film room, trying to figure out ways to get our outside linebackers (now they're called the Whip and Rover) to play deep, but we could never quite solve it.

Now that I had an opening on my staff, I wanted someone who could help me solve the problem. I talked to Wake Forest's John Gutekunst, who had coached at Tech under Bill Dooley, about coming back, but he declined. Coach Gutekunst would have done a great job — but when I looked a little further, I found the guy who understood the exact defense I had wanted to play for years.

That guy was Syracuse defensive backs coach Phil Elmassian, who had also been an assistant at Tech under Coach Dooley. When I contacted him, Elmo told me he had been studying this 4-3-4 package used by the University of Washington.

He said Washington's defense used a four-deep concept,

with the front line players in more of an attack-mode, charging up the field and making everything bounce to the sideline. When he described it to me, it sounded exactly like what Ron Zook and I had been looking for back in 1987.

It was an advanced form of that wide-tackle six. There were two tackles, two ends, the Mike, a Backer, a Whip, a Rover, two cornerbacks and a free safety.

The Backer and the Mike were the two inside linebackers. The Mike got his name because he was in the middle, and his main job is to stuff the run. The Backer has to be a little faster than the Mike, because he must sometimes cover the tight end down the middle of the field or a back in the flat.

The Whip and Rover were both kinda the same guy. The Whip needed to be fast, but he maybe not quite as nifty as the Rover. He might be a step slower. Today, we talk about our two corners, the free safety and the Rover as kind of being the same position. They all must be very, very fast.

This was the defense I was looking for. So, on Dec. 10th, I hired Elmo.

It was the most important hire I ever made.

It was important because he did more than just implement a new defense. He brought us a fiery temperament. In 1992, we couldn't hold a lead, and we needed something to shock the system. Elmo provided that. His hard-nosed personality and his confidence were changes we really needed. His personality was so different from everyone else we had around.

Hiring him was kinda a one-shot deal. He's such a competitive, smart guy, and he puts so much into it, that after a couple of years, he starts looking for a new challenge. I don't say that in a derogatory way. He's sort of a "my way or the highway" kinda guy, and that's not the way it always needs to be. But I have the highest regard for him. He was exactly what we needed in 1992.

In addition to Billy Hite and Bud Foster, who had been

with me since we got here in 1987 and who now run my offense and defense, there is another individual who has meant just as much to our success as Elmo being hired. His name is John Ballein, who is my administrative assistant.

John came on board as a graduate assistant during the summer prior to the 1987 season. The ironic thing is that I almost didn't hire him.

He had been a high school assistant at Western Branch in Chesapeake, Va., and had sent us a video resume.

At the time, John's hair was a lot longer than it is now and in the video he once even had a Mohawk hair cut. I just didn't think he would fit in.

But my defensive coordinator, Ron Zook, liked him and encouraged me to take a chance on him.

And I'm glad I did. He later became my administrative assistant in 1989.

Now, he helps me with almost every detail of our operation. And he's also a great racquetball and golfing partner.

Usually these days when I ask him about a specific detail, his frequent answer is: "Coach, it's already been taken care of."

Yet in 1992, there were more staff changes to come. In mid-December, Steve Marshall accepted the offensive line position at Tennessee. In January, I dismissed the two coaches I had reassigned, Mike Clark and Keith Jones, and hired J.B. Grimes from Arkansas, Rod Sharpless from Cornell and elevated graduate assistant Bryan Stinespring. I also reassigned Terry Strock from defensive ends to wide receivers and promoted quarterbacks coach Rickey Bustle to offensive coordinator.

Although Marshall, our offensive line coach, had been our offensive coordinator, I always thought the quarterbacks coach should call the plays. And Rickey was ready to be a coordinator. It was a good fit.

I felt lousy about having to fire those guys, but it was never personal. I'm still on good terms with all of them. It wasn't that they were bad coaches. They are good coaches, and they are good people.

But when you are ahead of seven teams in the fourth quarter and you can't put them away, there's a confidence factor involved, and sometimes you just need to do something different, regardless of what it is.

Here is an example of how we needed to do things better. One day we were in a recruiting meeting and we had a coach and he had his legs propped up on a desk and he said, "Frankie, I think we can get this kid."

I looked at the prospect's transcript. "He doesn't qualify," I said. "He doesn't have three maths."

"Yes he does, Frankie," the assistant said. "It's right here. Algebra, Calculus, Algebra II."

I looked at the transcript and didn't see it. "Show it to me," I said.

He got up and looked at my folder. "Oh," the coach said. "I was looking at the wrong transcript."

Well I kinda lost it right there. "This is the kinda thing I'm talking about!" I said.

We just had to go in another direction. We were running in one direction and getting close, but never getting there. We had to run in a different direction. That was it more than anything.

Stinespring was a great story. He was a graduate assistant for us and his wife, Shelley, was a secretary for us on the second floor. But Bryan's GA time had run out and he was planning to take a high school job as a vice-principal and coach football. I mean, he had it all set up, and Shelley was excited about it.

My assistant head coach, Billy Hite, was on top of this situation. Billy has always been my go-between guy. He keeps me up on what's going on.

"You've got to do something, coach, or we're going to lose him," Billy said. "And he's too good a coach to lose."

Shortly after talking to Billy I went to Bryan.

"Listen, I know you're ready to take this job, but I don't want to lose you," I said. "Write down a job title that makes sense, and I'll pay you $10 a hour to keep you here. And when there's an opening on my staff, I will hire you."

So Bryan stayed and became "Director of Sports Programs" at $10 an hour, because he believed what I had said. Another reason I wouldn't let him go was because his wife was such a great secretary.

Eventually, it worked out for Bryan to join my staff as an assistant coach.

Now it was the winter of 1993, and only Billy Hite, Bud Foster and Rickey Bustle remained from my original Tech staff. But even though we had made all of these changes, we still needed something else.

We had been so close to getting over the top, but because of those NCAA sanctions, we were always a few players short. So we kept playing a guy who might not quite be what we wanted personality-wise, because he was the best we had. We weren't sure the guy behind him could do the job. We were trying like heck to win games, so it became a real tough decision.

So do we cut loose this troublesome guy? Is the guy behind him ready to play? Can we afford to take that chance, with our jobs on the line?

What was the right thing to do? After those tough first two years we started to turn the thing around. Then we regressed. That's when not having those 33 guys we couldn't recruit came back to haunt us.

After I made those coaching changes, I met with my new staff and we scrutinized every single thing we did in our program. I said, "OK, why can't we finish a game? Why can't we get this thing done?"

And it always kept coming back to the same thing.

We needed discipline.

16

20 Key Steps to a Seven-Game Turnaround

AFTER MY childhood accident, my family didn't dwell on my misfortune. We just focused on what we needed to do to get me well. We tried to look at the positive side of things, and I think a lot of that mentality stayed with me the rest of my life.

When I'm actually in the middle of something, I'm aware of things, but I don't dwell on them. After that 2-8-1 season in 1992, people would tell me about something negative that was said on the radio, or something that was written in the paper, but I tried hard not to let it bother me. I asked my secretary then, Margaret Brown, to read the letters, and if it was a bad one, I told her to throw it away. Reading that stuff doesn't do anybody any good.

Instead, I thought, "What can I do to make this thing better?"

And one of the things I knew I could do was visit my old friend, Bobby Ross.

So I went to see Bobby, who was with the San Diego Chargers. They went 4-12 in 1991 under Dan Henning. The next year, under Bobby, they went 11-5 and won a playoff game.

"What did you do to turn things around?" I asked him.

"Frankie, you're a good enough coach," he said. "You don't really need to change a whole lot. But these are some of the things that have worked for us."

He gave me a list of suggestions. Here was a guy I really respected and trusted, and what he said really made sense. I went back and discussed them with my staff, and one thing led to another. These brainstorming sessions resulted in things we still do today. Changes that helped turn our program around. I'll share them with you now.

1. FRIDAY NIGHT VIDEO

This was one of the first things Bobby suggested. He told me about this video he put together and played the Saturday night before each game. It was a compilation video that just showed the positive plays from the week before.

Even in a bad game, you can always find 10 or 15 great plays somebody made. They might have made a great block, a great catch or a great move. You put those things together and watch it and it's amazing. If you hadn't seen the game, you'd think, "dadgum, this team is pretty good."

I remembered what Coach Claiborne said. He'd show a guy making a good play and he'd say, "If you can make that play once, you can make it every time." That always made sense to me. We began showing our players doing all of these great things and they began believing in themselves. The thing I really like about it is that we always put great blocks on that video. It is usually the only chance an offensive lineman has to get noticed.

It developed into a fun thing, watching all those great plays. I bet a lot of players would say it's the most fun they have each week, watching that video. The kids are screaming and laughing and having a great time. It loosens everybody up, and it motivates them to go out there and make great plays on Saturday.

2. PUNISHMENT

My key thought was, either our players do things right and be successful, or do it wrong and be punished, and get on with it. We have two types of punishments. One of them is the Wednesday Morning Sunrise Service with our strength and conditioning coach, Mike Gentry. Coach Gentry is an intense guy and you don't want to wake him up for a 6 a.m. drill.

The second type of punishment are Reminders, which are 40 seconds of up-downs, followed by 20 seconds of rest. When the position coach believes the player is sufficiently reminded, the drill ends.

Here's the point: I didn't want the punishment to be the key issue. In the past, one coach might have his players run the stadium steps; another might have guys doing pushups. It became a thing where the kids were dwelling more about WHAT they were doing, rather than WHY. The main issue wasn't what kind of punishment you got; the main issue was that you screwed up, and we didn't want you to do it again.

Now, the punishment is the same for everybody. If a player messed up something simple, he'd do Reminders. But if you missed study hall, or were late for a meeting on a game weekend, something serious, you got the Sunrise Service at 6 a.m. with Coach Gentry.

3. STUDY HALL HOURS

If you missed your study halls hours, you now had to make up that time on Sunday, plus you had the 6 a.m. Sunrise Service. We wanted our kids to go ahead and do it when they're supposed to, because if they don't, they're still going to have to put in those hours, plus deal with Coach Gentry.

4. ENFORCEABLE RULES

We simplified our rules into ones we could enforce. We used to have an 11 p.m. curfew every night. Then what happened was a kid had to go work on a school group project and would have to get permission to stay later. Those study sessions could go on late. That 11 p.m. curfew became something that was tough to enforce. So we simplified it.

We said, "look, we're going to treat you like men." The only two nights we had curfew were Thursday and Friday nights, the two key nights before a game.

We said, "now look, if you have to be out of your room to study or write a paper, do it on Sunday through Wednesday. But if we call you on Thursday, you better talk to us on the phone."

We'd pick one set of rooms to check each week. One week it could be an apartment complex; the next might be the dormitory. And while one coach was doing that, other coaches will make some random calls. You never knew when it would be, but when it happened, you had better be there.

My whole point was: "If we say it, it's going to happen. We mean it." There was none of this, "well, they might break this one." We didn't put in a lot of rules, but the ones we have, we enforce without discussion.

5. KINDRED SPIRIT

This went back to my coaching days at the Citadel. Those kids moaned and groaned about it while they were there, but they were the most loyal people. They all went through something tough and became better for it. So, on game weekends, we'd all wear a tie on the flight. When we all got to the hotel, they all had to wear our Virginia Tech warmup suit. If they were going to wear a hat, it was going to be a Virginia Tech hat. I wanted everybody to get into the mindset that we were on a mission together.

6. LOOK THE SAME IN PRACTICE

I remember back in 1987, when we went down to play South Carolina. We went out on Williams-Brice Stadium for our Friday walk-through. We were wearing these old ratty gray sweats that had numbers marked through three or four times in black magic marker. When we're done with our workout we passed the Gamecocks coming onto the field, and they were all wearing shiny new black sweat suits.

I remember going up to our equipment manager, Lester Karlin.

"Lester," I said, "We've got to get us some new sweats."

Also, in past practices, our players would all wear different colored shirts under their workout gear. After 1992, the only colors we allowed on our practice field were Hokie colors. And when you hit that gate at practice, you started jogging. There was no walking. Shirt-tails were tucked in, too. I wanted everybody to take pride in the way they looked in their uniform. When you're relaxing around campus, you can have your shirt-tail out. But when you're on this practice field, things are different. We have the best gear you could possibly have here at Virginia Tech, and I want you to look good. And if you look good, you will take pride in yourself and you will play better. If you look sloppy, you might play sloppy.

7. DRESS SQUAD ONLY TRAVELS

The only people who travel with us on the road or dress at home are those who have a chance to play in the ballgame. In 1992 I remember some people telling me that we had players talking to friends in the stands during games. I had my headset on and I was involved in the game, so I had no idea.

When they told me that, I couldn't believe it. It was just incredible to me. So we eliminated taking any player on the road who didn't have a legitimate shot of playing in the game.

If a guy doesn't think he's going to play, he doesn't have that nervousness in his stomach and he might be goofing around at the pregame meal, laughing. I want everybody in the same frame of mind.

8. MONDAY MORNING VIDEO

The NCAA requires that Sunday or Monday be a free time for players. We chose Sunday. What we started doing was get our kids over here to watch film of Saturday's game at 7 a.m. on Monday. They could come in on Sunday if they wanted to, but that was their choice. This was good because it got our kids up and going on Monday morning and then go from that movie session to class.

9. PENALIZED FOR PENALTIES

At the team meeting Monday afternoon, we started showing clips of every penalty. Before, we used to run a guy 100 yards for every yard of the infraction, but we still seemed to keep getting penalties. So what I started doing was taking those penalties, and putting them on a video, and showing them at our Monday meeting.

Now, in front of the whole group, they're sitting there watching a guy slug somebody late, or clip a guy in the back. In 1992, we were penalized 88 times for 755 yards. Once we started showing those in front of the whole team, let me tell you, it cut down on that stuff. You rarely see us hit a guy out of bounds anymore. You put that peer pressure on them, showing them that they're hurting the whole football team, and it puts it in a whole different light. That was one of the better things we did.

10. FINISH PRACTICE, OR RISE

It's never good for morale when some of your players are working their butts off in practice and others aren't. Sometimes guys might be a little sore, and they might beg out of a drill.

So this is what we started doing: If for any reason you dropped out of any practice or conditioning period, you had to see the trainer at 6:15 the next morning. If the guys are legitimately hurt, we of course want them in for therapy.

But if you're treading that thin line where your hamstring might be a little sore and you're thinking about dropping out, maybe you might think, "If I do that, I have to get treatment at 6:15 tomorrow morning."

11. NO FIGHTING

To understand this one, you have to go way back to when I was a player. It was the last Saturday scrimmage of spring practice, and it wasn't a very good practice. Coach Claiborne announced that a select few would not have to practice on Monday — I was lucky enough to be one of them — but the rest had to practice on Monday, and it was going to be a "get-after-it" session. And when Coach Claiborne said it was going to be a "get-after-it" session, you went, "aw, geez, here we go."

So Monday came and after one of the first plays, a big fight broke out. People were hostile and flying around and the hitting was great. But every few plays, a big fight would break out. It was the darndest scrimmage you'd ever seen. And after the scrimmage, Coach Claiborne said, "That was one of the best, most spirited practices we've ever had here at Virginia Tech."

As a coach you always want your kids' motor running, with a refuse-to-lose attitude. So when I was coaching, if we'd have a fight break out, sometimes we'd let them fight it out before breaking it up. Then we had that problem in Louisville where our defensive end got in a fight and it cost us a game, and I started thinking, "this fighting stuff is killing us."

We now stress that the reason we practice is to help each other get better, not to beat each other up. The defensive guy should respect the fact that the offensive lineman is going to do everything in his power to protect the quarterback. You need to be violent from the time the ball is snapped to when the whistle blows. But when the whistle blows, stop. We preached intelligent recklessness. Do not hit people out of bounds. Don't hit people in the back. And don't fight. If you fight, you get Reminders afterward.

12. AWARDS

We started giving out awards after a game, but we only do it after a win. If we lose, we don't hand out awards. The Lane Stadium playing field is named after Wes Worsham, and he comes into our dressing room to hand out a game ball to the guy he thinks played best.

But we also started allowing our captains to present the offensive, defensive, and special teams game balls. And those are some great moments.

In 1999, when Billy Hite's wife, Anne, was in the hospital, the captains gave Billy the offensive game ball. Many times, someone will get the game ball and he'll say, "no, I think another guy deserves it." Sometimes a guy will get a game ball and his remarks to the team will be just exactly what needs to be said.

It's a deal where players are sharing with each other, communicating with each other.

My best times in sports are in that dressing room. When we started giving out those awards right after a win, it did a lot to bring our teams together. Your captains, your senior leadership, get to have a little bit more say in your program, and the coaching staff and players get closer.

13. WARNING HORN

It always drove me nuts to have players late to practice. And it drove other players nuts, too, because they were on time. So two minutes before we started flexing, we blew a horn. And if you weren't on the field, you knew you better be moving. If not, you meet Coach Gentry for his Sunrise Service.

14. BEST VS. BEST IN PRACTICE

In that 2-8-1 season of 1992, it seemed like we never got any better as the season went on. Our first team used to work a good 45 or 50 minutes against the scout team during team periods. But after about 15 minutes the scout team would start getting tired, and we would get diminishing returns on our drills. It wasn't realistic and nobody was getting better.

So we started putting in a 10-minute period of our first team offense against our first team defense in true game speed. It might not be the defense we'd be facing that week, but they were facing good people. We don't block below the waist or tackle to the ground during that period, but all the action before that is full speed.

Then we run the scout team for 10 minutes. Work on formations, motion and different assignments. Then we come back for another 10 minutes going against the first-teamers again. The scout team stayed fresh, and I started seeing us getting better as the season went on.

This was a big change from what we had been doing. We used to be worried that we might have too many injuries, going best vs. best like that.

That, however, wasn't the big consideration. Instead, it was not working against the particular offense or defense we were going to see that week. But the positives we got from it outweighed anything else.

15. MIDDLE DRILL

Virginia Tech has always been known for having tough football players. But that 2-8-1 year, we became a soft team. We weren't very deep, so we never went full speed in practice in the fall, as far as tackling guys to the ground.

But after that year, we decided that every Tuesday we'd have a middle drill, seven-on-seven.

Billy Hite used to talk about Bill Dooley's old offense, "Hi Diddle Diddle, We're Coming Up The Middle." Well, that says it all about this drill.

We were taking on blockers full speed, ballcarriers taking on tacklers full speed. We call it "game speed." It gave us a toughness we were missing.

The funny thing was, the drill seemed to pick up the rest of the practice.

16. THE UPS AND DOWNS OF FUMBLING

Fumbling the ball is really just a matter of concentration. Before, when a kid fumbled in practice, we'd yell, "Hey! Don't fumble!" But that just didn't seem to work.

So we started doing a thing where, whenever there was a fumble in practice, we'd take all 11 guys who were on the field over and do up-downs for a few seconds. It became a team deal. So we immediately gave the kids reinforcement that you don't turn the ball over. When you make an issue of it, it helps to keep the players focused.

17. SAME SCHEDULE EVERY WEEK

I'm a special teams fanatic, and each day I'd figure out what we needed to work on in practice that day. It would always vary from day to day, depending on what I wanted to do. Then we'd build the rest of the practice around that.

Well, that messed up my offensive and defensive coordinators, because they had to wait on me before devising their practice schedules. They didn't know how many periods they had to work.

My heart was in the right place. I wanted to make sure we were stressing special teams, but it was probably screwing up some other things. So we changed that.

Now, we have the same schedule every week. They know ahead of time exactly what we're going to do, and we're much better organized. Our Monday practice is exactly the same. Tuesday is different from Monday, but it is the same every Tuesday. And so on. My coordinators can do their team scripts a week in advance.

18. DELEGATE RESPONSIBILITY

One of the things Bobby Ross told me when I visited him was, "hire the right guys, and let them coach." You hear that a lot, but when Bobby told me that I really took it to heart.

I used to be involved with every aspect of the team, but now, the offense belongs to Rickey Bustle and the defense belongs to Bud Foster. They are both great coordinators, and what I've found is that they both feel responsible for their respective game plans.

We've been together a long time and share the same philosophy, so I trust them. And I'm in charge of special teams. I really think it's the most effective way of operation. I stay out of those meeting rooms now.

It's funny; it seems like the less I coach, the more we win.

19. RECRUITING ACCOUNTABILITY

Three coaches have to sign off on a kid before we recruit him: The recruiting coach, the position coach and then myself.

This allows the position coach to get an idea of what's there. He can start to rank the kids in a particular position. So if the position coach signs off on the kid, it means he fills a spot in the order.

I keep the records in a big binder.

In the old days, when we were talking about personnel, a kid's name would come up and someone would ask, "why did we recruit him?" And the position coach would say, "I didn't WANT him." But now I can say, "hey, wait a minute," and go back to that book, and I can say, "all right, I'm going to read your comments here." That makes everybody accountable.

We also keep a score sheet for each coach. They get points depending on how their recruits turn out.

The scoring sheet goes like this: If a player earns a letter in his first year, the coach gets 6 points. Second year: 4 points. Third year: 2 points. Fourth year: 1 point. Fifth year: 0 points.

On the other hand, if a player fails to letter in his first year, the coach gets 0 points. Second year, -1. Third year, -2. Fourth year, -4. Fifth year, -6.

If a player takes a medical hardship because of injury, the coach gets -3.

If a player flunks out, quits the program, transfers or is dismissed, the coach is docked -10. The coach is also penalized if the university or law enforcement officials take action against a player.

Coaches also get points if a player they recruited receives honors:

First Team Big East: 5 points.
Second Team Big East: 3 points.
Team captain: 10 points.
Makes a pro team: 10 points.
All-America: 8 points.
Wins any Tech football banquet award: 7 points.

A coach also gets docked three points per GPA or hours short that forces a player to go to summer school.

A coach gets one point for every start his player makes. And he gets 10 points for every walk-on who earns a scholarship.

This makes things fun and competitive, but the big reason for it is accountability. And it keeps them from going out and trying to sign 10 guys for the sake of signing 10 guys.

20. GET YOUR REST

Those early years, we worked ourselves to death. We'd never stop to eat breakfast or lunch. It was all business.

The Tuesday before our very first ballgame, against

Clemson in 1987, I got a little nervous and wanted to make sure all the details were taken care of. So I asked the defensive staff to stay up late to discuss some of the stuff they were doing, and then we were back in there at 6 a.m.

My defensive coordinator, Ron Zook, came to me and said, "Look, we just cannot do this."

I knew he was right, but I was just trying to check every detail.

So that changed. Our new deal was that we do our job, go home, get our rest, and come in fresh. There were a couple of days in April, during the middle of spring drills, where I got the whole staff over at Blacksburg Country Club for a few rounds of golf. I didn't care what people would think if they saw our coaches out having fun on the course during spring drills. You've got to have a life and have some fun. When you do that, everybody's mind is clear and the whole day is more efficient.

So that was how, one year after going 2-8-1, we went 9-3 and won the Independence Bowl.

17

THE BIG PAYBACK

I KNEW WE had good players and coaches. The 1993 season was time to turn up the wick and prove it.

Everybody expected us to beat Bowling Green in the opener. The real pressure came the next week, at Pittsburgh. I don't know if it was ever said, but I got the feeling it was sort of a "win or else" type game.

The Panthers were coming off a 14-10 upset at Southern Mississippi and the game was considered a tossup. But we had a school-record 675 yards of total offense and won, 63-21.

I rarely involve myself in the offensive and defensive conversations going on in the headset during the game. But that game was one time when I felt compelled to speak up.

For a while now, assistant coach Bryan Stinespring had been bugging offensive coordinator Rickey Bustle to let him call a play during a game.

We had just had a series where we ran it something like 13 consecutive times. We had hammered it down the field and were getting ready to score.

Rickey then clicked over to Bryan and asked him what he wanted to do. Pittsburgh had stacked the line so Bryan said, "I think we should throw it."

Well, we had 500 yards rushing that day. I got on the headset and screamed, "we just drove down the field running the ball at will, and you want to THROW it?"

All I heard was a click. It was the sound of Bryan turning off his microphone. I don't think he tried calling a play for two years after that.

The Pittsburgh game set the tone for the 1993 season. We finished ranked No. 11 in scoring offense and won nine games. Center Jim Pyne was a unanimous all-American. We were undefeated at home. We finished the season ranked No. 20 in the USA Today/CNN coaches' poll and No. 22 by The Associated Press.

Our only losses were to third-ranked Miami in the Orange Bowl, No. 22 West Virginia in Morgantown by one point, and Boston College.

Miami was just too quick for us. We could only manage 176 yards of total offense and lost, 21-2. But we were getting closer.

We almost beat West Virginia but missed a 44-yard field goal with 1:10 to play. The ball was heading straight for the goalposts but veered off. Six years later, on that same field, we had a late field goal go our way from just about the same distance, but going the opposite way. But it wasn't to be this season and we lost, 14-13.

After beating East Carolina, 31-12, on October 30th, we were 6-2 and cracked the AP Top 25 for the first time with me as head coach. The next game, Boston College hammered us,

48-34. The BC quarterback, Glenn Foley was 21 of 29 for 448 yards. He just killed us.

About the fourth play of the game, defensive coordinator Phil Elmassian said, "We can't stop 'em," and threw off his headset.

I thought, "Aw, geez. We've got a lot of plays left."

But we won our last two games in a big way. We had Syracuse at home, and I brought Coach Claiborne in to say a few words to the team before that game. It might have helped, because we beat Syracuse, 45-24. He was also there for the 1990 Virginia game, so he had a pretty good record going there.

What a day that was. Seniors Joe Swarm, John Burke and Chris Barry dumped a Gatorade cooler full of water over me on the sideline. It was my first victory shower. I got that photograph blown up and framed and it still hangs in my office. In the dressing room, the Independence Bowl extended an invitation, and we happily accepted. We really needed that.

What a sigh of relief. We had been close before. We just needed to go to a bowl game, because that's the way you are judged in this business.

The next week we went to Charlottesville and beat No. 23 Virginia, 20-17. It was the first time Tech had won in Charlottesville since I became head coach. We finished the regular season 8-3 and ranked No. 22 by The Associated Press. Then we began preparing for No. 20 Indiana in the Independence Bowl.

Since then we've been to the Sugar Bowl twice, the Gator Bowl twice, the Orange Bowl and the Music City Bowl. All of those were great trips. But that Independence Bowl was the greatest bowl trip we've ever taken, because everything was new. We had nothing to compare it too, so everything seemed great.

John Ballein and Sharon McCloskey fixed up the locker room with orange and maroon balloons, streamers and pom-

poms. They didn't have one of those helium tanks, so they blew up those balloons the hard way.

I'll never forget that day. It was New Year's Eve in Shreveport, La., and the game was televised on ESPN. It was a sunny afternoon, perfect for football; we were facing a team from the Big Ten, and a great many of the fans in the stands were Hokies.

We led, 14-13, with 35 seconds left in the half. Indiana had the ball at midfield, threatening to score.

Their quarterback, John Paci, went back to pass, and senior Whip linebacker DeWayne Knight blitzed from the right side. He lost his footing and dove at Paci's feet. Paci stepped forward to avoid him and ran into our middle linebacker, George DelRicco, who wrapped his arms around him.

Paci then cocked his arm to get rid of the ball when Knight scrambled up and popped him, knocking the ball loose. Defensive tackle J.C. Price tried to pick up the ball, but it bounced into the hands of linebacker Lawrence Lewis, who caught it on the dead run and sprinted 20 yards for a touchdown.

Now there were 23 seconds left.

Our ensuing kickoff was a little short, and Indiana returned it 38 yards to our 42. Paci then completed a nine-yard pass to the left sideline, and time expired.

As we were trotting off the field, I saw Hoosier coach Bill Mallory arguing with the officials. He claimed they called timeout and there should be one second left on the clock.

"No way," I thought. I tried to get our players off the field, in an effort to influence the officials' decision.

It didn't work. The officials put one second back on the clock and waved us back.

"We're on national TV, and you guys are losing control of the game!" I yelled to the officials on the way back to the sideline. "What do you think all those people watching are thinking?"

Indiana set up to attempt a 51-yard field goal. They snapped the ball and defensive tackle Jeff Holland fought through the center of the line and tipped the kick. It flew high in the air, and returner Antonio Banks settled under it at our 20-yard line.

He started to his right, then reversed his field as a wall of blockers formed.

At about the 15-yard line, Torrian Gray unloaded on an Indiana player, knocking him back about five yards on his rear end. Banks scored untouched, the half ended, and we had a 28-13 lead, and that was pretty much the ballgame.

"Great call!" I yelled to the officials as we went off the field. "I guess you guys really ARE keeping control of this game!"

Cornerback Tyronne Drakeford intercepted a pass in that game, which was a great story because he had broken his leg in our seventh game of the season. He was a tough kid. He wasn't highly recruited, but he worked hard. Before the 1994 NFL draft, a lot of Tech fans were wondering where he would get drafted.

"He wouldn't get drafted into the Army," Elmassian said.

This time Elmassian was wrong. The San Francisco 49ers drafted Drakeford in the second round, and he's still in the NFL.

We beat Indiana, 45-20, and as soon as he hit the dressing room Jim Pyne grabbed a bottle of champagne, popped it and started dumping it over everybody's head.

Virginia Governor George Allen joined us in the dressing room and we were afraid Pyne was going to douse him, too. The governor was wearing an orange-and-maroon tie and put on a Virginia Tech hat, which was interesting, because he was a University of Virginia graduate.

But today, he wanted to be a Hokie.

18

RECRUITING: WAR STORIES FROM THE ROAD

WINNING THE Independence Bowl really gave our recruiting a boost. That winter we signed what, at the time, was regarded as our best class ever. It included quarterback Al Clark, offensive linemen Gennaro DiNapoli, Derek Smith, Dwight Vick and Todd Washington, linebacker Tony Morrison and tailbacks Marcus Parker and Ken Oxendine.

Smith turned down West Virginia and Penn State. Morrison and Oxendine were both ranked among the Top Five players in the state, and we beat Virginia for both of them.

Oxendine was a big one for us. Phil Elmassian did a heck of a job recruiting him. Ox's final four schools were Tennessee, Virginia, Georgia and Tech. In the end it came down to Virginia and us.

Ox was trying to make his decision and called Billy Hite. "I just talked to Terry Kirby," he said. Kirby was a great tailback for Virginia.

"Why did you do that?" Billy said.

"The coaches at Virginia told me to call him."

"Well, I'm going to tell you who you need to call," Billy said. "You need to call Vaughn Hebron."

Vaughn had been a big recruit for us. He was a great tailback; he just had trouble staying healthy. The thing with Vaughn, though, was his personality. He had a great smile and had a great sense of humor. He was the kind of guy you just liked being around.

I guess Ox called Vaughn, because a little bit later, I got a call from him. It was the day of the Super Bowl and we were having a little party.

"Coach, I've made up my mind," Ox said.

"Great."

"It was a tough decision, though."

"I'm sure it was."

"Well, I just wanted to let you know, OK?"

"Fine. Uh, Ken, where are you going?"

"Oh. I'm coming to Tech, coach."

Derek Smith turned out to be a great offensive lineman for us. Bryan Stinespring and I went up to his family's house in West Virginia on a recruiting trip, and his mom, Rosemary, had made all kinds of food. I'm talking about 27 pies. It was something.

I was dressed in one of my nicest suits and I sat down in the living room. Well, the Smiths had a beagle who liked to jump up and sit in your lap.

Bryan was dressed up, too: turtleneck, sport coat, hair all gelled up, and he didn't want that dog anywhere near him. But the dog took a real liking to me.

"Don't ya'll mind that dog, now," Rosemary said while I was eating a piece of pie.

"Oh, I've got a beagle like this at home," I said. "His name is Jock. I love dogs."

This beagle was getting hair all over the place. I think it shed while it walked. I was sitting there holding a plate of lemon meringue, and the dog was licking me. Hair was all over my pants. It looked like I was wearing flannel.

"Is that dog bothering you?" Rosemary said.

"Oh, the dog is fine, Mrs. Smith," I said. "I love dogs. He's just like Jock."

After awhile it was time to leave. We walked outside and Bryan said, "Coach, you did a heck of a job in there today."

"Coach Stinespring," I said, "will you do me a favor?"

"What is it, coach?"

"Remind me to get rid of Jock when I get home."

One thing for sure, recruiting trips can get a little crazy. One year when I was at Murray State we were recruiting this really good player from Knoxville, a defensive back named James (Squeaky) Yarborough. We had a volunteer coach who was learning the trade, and let me tell you he worked like heck. He got involved in recruiting this player. He had some kind of a connection, so he drove me down there to see Squeaky.

Well, he got turned around in Knoxville and pretty soon we were lost. We ended up being about 45 minutes late for our appointment with this kid.

As we got out of the car I told him, "Son, if I were paying you anything at all, I'd fire you."

It worked out, though. We got Squeaky.

In the winter of 1999 Bryan Stinespring and I were in Tidewater, recruiting Keith Willis. He was a good basketball player, too, and then-Tech head basketball coach Bobby Hussey was interested in him, too.

We were there all day long; we visited Norview High School, went to his basketball game that night, everything. After the game the plan was to meet Keith at his house and meet his parents, Keith and Mara. It was about 9:30 at night and we were driving through downtown Norfolk. On the way, something dawned on me.

"I don't know if I can see him," I said.

"Why not?" Bryan said.

"I think Bobby Hussey has already had a home visit with him. I don't know if the NCAA allows me a home visit, too."

Bryan wasn't sure that was the case.

"What I'M saying is, I don't know if I can see him," I said.

So Bryan got on the cell phone and called John Ballein and told him the situation.

"Let me call Tim Parker," John said. Tim is our compliance officer, but he wasn't at home. So John drove to the office to get the NCAA rulebook. He was going to call us back when he found the answer.

Bryan and I were driving around in Norfolk, killing time. Well, Bryan will be the first one to tell you he's the worst driver in America.

"Pull this darn car over," I said, looking at him. "You're making me nervous."

He pulled over into somebody's driveway, and I could tell Bryan was getting a little frustrated. "Coach, what do you want to do here?" he said.

"This is what we're going to do," I said. "You go to the Willis house. I don't want to sit here on private property; is there a public place around?"

"There's a 7-Eleven a few lights away, in downtown," Bryan said, "but be careful. It's kinda a rough area."

"OK," I said. "I'll go there and wait for John to call me back."

I dropped Bryan off at the Willis' house. He went up and knocked on the door and went inside, and I drove over to the 7-Eleven, which was down the street.

I waited and there and all of a sudden I see this big man

dressed in black walking over to my car. He was about 6-foot-8. An imposing figure.

When he tapped on the window, I quickly lowered it.

"Frank Beamer?" he said.

"Yes," I said.

"Keith Willis Senior," he said.

Mr. Willis then told me that Bryan had been making small talk at the Willis house and told him about our situation.

"Wait a minute," Mr. Willis told Bryan. "You're telling me that Frank Beamer's here to see my kid? Well then he's coming inside my house. I'm going to go get Frank Beamer. Where is he?"

"He's at the 7-Eleven," Bryan said.

"I'm going to go get Frank Beamer," he said.

Ten minutes later, Mr. Willis came back to see Bryan.

"Did you see coach?" Bryan said.

"I saw him," Mr. Willis said, kind of giggling.

"What's the matter?" Bryan said.

"The coach wanted to sign me up for a scholarship, too."

Turns out it was OK for me to make a home visit; we just were allowed one less evaluation period.

We got Keith, but not all recruiting trips end in success.

One year I met assistant coach Charley Wiles down in Florida. We were to see this high school player who was a big-time safety prospect. We arrived at the young man's house about 5 p.m. His mother was in the kitchen cooking dinner, but the kid was nowhere around.

"My son's not home yet," she said. "He's at an all-star practice. He should be back around 8."

We left to get something to eat and returned at 8, and the young man still wasn't there. We waited around till 9:30 p.m., and he still had not showed up. Charley was determined to see this player. We had eaten something like three times while we were waiting, and I was getting a little upset.

"I've gained ten pounds already," I said, looking at Charley, "and I still haven't seen this young man."

We went back to the house around 11:45 p.m., and by then the father was in there with a bunch of kids from the neighborhood, working scholarship deals for them, too. This went on till about 1:30 in the morning. It was a total fiasco.

We finally left the house and Charley apologized for how everything got so out of whack. He was really sorry about it.

"Sometimes those things happen," I said. "Let's move on."

We both ended up laughing about it.

That was a long day. I remember another trip to Florida being a little shorter.

Rickey Bustle was recruiting this big prospect from Tampa. It was between N.C. State and us. We drove to the kid's house, made a little small talk in the living room then his mother says, "well sit down."

My back had barely hit the chair when the kid says, "I'm going to N.C. State."

Well, I stood right back up and turned to Rickey and said, "OK, let's go!"

Rickey was upset and went storming out to the rental car. He thought the window was down and threw his briefcase at it. The briefcase slammed against the glass and fell to the ground. But hey, sometimes those things happen. If a kid doesn't want to come, he doesn't want to come.

Sometimes WE don't want a kid to come to Virginia Tech. I tell our players, "If a guy doesn't fit in here, let me know the Sunday morning of his visit, before I meet with him."

Several years ago we got a visit from a very good linebacker prospect. Sunday morning his host comes to me and says, "this kid is a jerk. We don't need him." That was good enough for me. I didn't offer him a grant.

I believe you recruit human beings. You recruit personalities. Sure, they must have a certain talent level. And you had better get yourself a couple of game-changers. But after that, you recruit personalities. We want people who buy into our philosophy. We want people who want to be at Virginia Tech, who will work like heck to become better.

Take a guy like Michael Hawkes. He sort of epitomizes a lot of guys who have come through our program. When we recruit, we look at the person. What does football mean to him?

We look for people who love the game. Then we match them with our strength and conditioning coach, Mike Gentry. In my opinion he's the best in the country. We get these kids working with Mike and they develop. Maybe they weren't a highly recruited guy out of high school, but when they leave the program they might be a NFL prospect. We work a little bit harder than most places, and we get a little bit better results than most places.

Recruiting is a funny thing anyway. The "experts" rating these classes have never seen most of these kids play. It's impossible. They must go by what they hear, and they look at the schools recruiting the kid.

If we're recruiting a guy, he might be a three-star recruit. But when Notre Dame or Michigan starts recruiting the same guy, he might shoot up to four-star status. It goes around in a circle. So, in the end, all those guys at Notre Dame, at Florida, Florida State, Michigan are going to be rated highly.

That's why I don't put a lot of stock in how the experts rate a class. What I put stock in is the group of kids. If, at the end of the recruiting process, you feel really good about the players you have, then it has a chance to come out well down the road.

It seems like, every year, we've finished higher than we've been picked in the Big East for the past seven seasons.

Another reason for our success is our philosophy — from the first day — of recruiting the commonwealth of Virginia. We include Washington D.C. and Baltimore in that. We emphasize those areas. We believe it is critical to recruit well in your home state.

A great recent example of this is tight end Browning Wynn. He's from tiny Jonesville, Va. He came up here as a walk-on, he worked hard, we put him on scholarship, and he earned the highest possible award Mike Gentry gives in the weight room. He is a heck of a good athlete, but nobody was recruiting him out of his home state. There was no reason why he shouldn't be at Virginia Tech. Physically, he can really be something.

Of course, you've got to get some game-changers, and we were fortunate to have one of those in our home state in Michael Vick. There really wasn't a big recruiting story about him. His high school coach, Tommy Reamon, really cares about his players. He is a smart guy — he knows what is going on and kept the recruiting process on the up and up. In the end, you were either going to recruit Hampton's Ronald Curry or Warwick's Michael Vick. We cast our vote with Vick and Virginia cast its with Curry.

Recruiting is not very scientific, I'll tell you that.

These kids are at a time in their lives when there is a lot of changing going on. Physically they're changing. And they're changing the way they live, because they've been at home all these years and now they are going away to school. They're on their own, and it depends on how they adjust to that. There is a lot of stuff going on and to me, knowing as much about that guy as you can is the key issue. And the way you know a lot about them is to go back and recruit at the same high schools year after year.

After we played for the national championship, people asked me if we were going to increase our recruiting areas. I said, if anything, we were going to tighten them down. The rules only allow you to evaluate a kid only so many times. You can only know so much about him, the way the rules are.

So you need to rely on the words of somebody you trust,

and you build trust over time, going back to the same schools year after year.

The coaches can tell you if the kid is going to school every day, or if he works hard in the weight room, or how he reacts when it gets down to the tough times. Will the kid be with you then? That's another reason why it is critical to keep your coaching staff together. They've built up relationships with these high school coaches and they trust them.

That's how, even after that awful 2-8-1 season in 1992, we were able to get a player of the caliber of defensive end Cornell Brown. We had the foundation in place. We had a reputation for being honest people who cared about our players academically and that we treated kids right.

Cornell Brown could have gone anywhere he wanted to. And I think that's why we get a lot of brother combinations. Joe and Billy Swarm, Todd and T.J. Washington. And we very nearly signed Shawn Witten's brother, Jason, who had grown up in Tennessee as a lifelong Volunteers fan.

It really shouldn't have been a tough decision, but I think it says a lot about our program that Jason Witten strongly considered Virginia Tech before going with Tennessee this past winter.

I'll never forget when Cornell made his decision. He called a big press conference at E.C. Glass High School. It was between Virginia and us, and it really could have gone either way. Cornell sat down at the table and leaned toward the microphone and said:

"I'm going to the University of Virginia ... Tech."

He kind of had us going there for a split second. When he heard the news, I think Rickey Bustle started to cry.

Later, John Ballein asked Cornell why he announced his decision that way.

"Were you trying to have some fun with us, or what?" John said.

"No," Cornell said. "At the time, that's what I thought the school was called."

Cornell became part of a tradition of fast, game-breaking defensive ends at Virginia Tech. Corey Moore and John Engelberger were like that, and I think we have a guy now, Nathaniel Adibi, who could really be special.

When he came to campus for his official visit, I told my staff, "now, when you meet him, don't call him 'Nate' or 'Nat.' His name is 'Nathaniel.' This is very important." So when he came to meet our coaches, they were all afraid to talk to him, for fear of saying his name wrong. Bud Foster went to shake his hand and said, "I hope you have a good time!" and left.

Nathaniel was highly recruited. He was the kid that everyone said we wouldn't get. He was the total package: Big, strong, fast, great student, great family, great personality.

Like Michael, he's the type of kid who helps get you to the next level.

19

THE NEXT
LEVEL

I HAD GONE four years without making a coaching change, but now, for the third consecutive season, I was faced with the task of finding a new member of my staff. In January 1994, offensive coordinator Rickey Bustle accepted an offer to become offensive coordinator at the University of South Carolina.

I couldn't blame him. He's from Summerville, S.C., and was offered a big raise. We parted on good terms.

I brought in Gary Tranquill, who had been coaching quarterbacks for the Cleveland Browns under Bill Belichick. I had become familiar with him when he was part of George Welsh's staff at Virginia and had great respect for him.

There were big expectations in 1994. We were picked anywhere from No. 17, (*Lindy's*) to No. 25 (*The Sporting News*).

We started the season 4-0 and redeemed ourselves defensively at Boston College, winning a hard-fought game, 12-7. The win elevated Tech to No. 12 in the USA Today poll and No. 14 in AP, tying our highest AP ranking ever (in 1954).

Next was West Virginia in Blacksburg for a big ESPN Thursday night broadcast.

The campus was buzzing that whole week. Students were camping outside of Cassell Coliseum for tickets, so I bought them a bunch of pizzas. I wanted to reward them for their loyalty.

We played great and won, 34-6. After the game, USA Today ran a big story on us on the front cover of its sports section, calling us the "Big East boom team." On the lower right hand corner of the front page, they ran a story on another Hokie, baseball manager Johnny Oates, who is a good friend of mine. It was unusual to have two Hokies side-by-side on the front page of the USA Today sports section. The story on Johnny, however, wasn't necessarily good news about Johnny, and I felt for him.

Dating back to 1993, we had a seven-game winning streak going. Syracuse snapped it the following week as we lost, 28-20, in the Carrier Dome, after we led going into the fourth quarter.

We then won our next three and were ranked No. 10 before facing No. 4 Miami in the Orange Bowl. They had Warren Sapp and Ray Lewis and were just too quick for us and we lost, 24-3.

During the game, when our quarterback dropped back to throw it looked like there was a race to see if he would be able to set up before Sapp got there. Sometimes, I'm not sure Sapp didn't beat him there.

Lewis, who was just a sophomore, had something like 18 tackles that afternoon.

After the game, I told reporters, "I think this is our best

football team, but we're still not at Miami's level. We're still a recruiting class or two away from that."

We beat Rutgers, 41-34, but they outscored us, 21-0, in the fourth quarter and we had to recover an onside kick with 1:54 left to seal the win.

We were ranked No. 11 in the coaches' poll. Next was No. 14 Virginia for the regular season finale. It was the first time both teams had been ranked in the Top 20 at the time of the game.

Our seniors remembered that 1990 finale against Virginia when we wore all-maroon outfits and wanted to do something special, too, so we came out in orange jerseys and orange pants.

We played awful. Virginia was ranked No. 1 nationally against the run. We were forced to throw and our senior quarterback, Maurice DeShazo, had a tough day. He threw five interceptions, but he also had completed a lot of passes. It seemed like every pass was either a completion or an interception. Somebody was catching everything.

After about the third interception, Coach Tranquill said, "Frank, I'm thinking about pulling Maurice and giving Jim Druckenmiller some work."

"Nah, I'll tell you what," I said. "Maurice has taken us this far. It's his last home game. Leave him in there."

About two more interceptions later, I got on the headset.

"Tranq," I said, "I think you're right. Let's pull him."

"Hell no, not now," Tranq said. "I think there's some kind of record we can break."

We finished with eight turnovers and gained only 33 yards on the ground. And let me tell you, that was the end of those all-orange uniforms. I don't know where they are now, but after the way Virginia hammered us, I never want to see them again.

We had begun experimenting with orange pants in 1993. We had worn them with white jerseys and once even with maroon jerseys. But I was always a guy who felt like our base color was maroon, and you worked orange in as trim. Orange was a secondary color.

Now we wear maroon jerseys and white pants at home, and white-on-white on the road. We were spending too much time on what we were going to wear on Saturday instead of how we were going to play. Now there are no big decisions to make.

Our uniforms have become more and more basic over the years. We took the stripes off the white pants in 1994; we took the stripes off the jersey sleeves and replaced them with orange numerals in 1996; and finally, we took the stripes off the helmets in 1998.

The helmet change wasn't my idea. I always kind of liked those stripes on there. Senior cornerback Loren Johnson headed up the change. He was the one who was brave enough to come in my office and propose it. My deal was, "if you guys want it, and you think it's right, then we'll do it."

Communication is a key, key part of having a good football team. If my players feel a certain way, I want them to say it. And if I have something I want to say, I'm going to say that, too. We might agree, we might disagree, but we'll talk about it, and you won't need an appointment. If I'm here, come on in and we'll sit down and talk. We're in this thing together. We want our players to have good lives and we want them to win games.

Despite the Virginia game, we earned a bid to the Gator Bowl to face Tennessee. It was the biggest bowl in our school's history: A $1.5 million payout, eighth among all bowls.

"This is the greatest thing that has ever happened to Virginia Tech's football program," athletic director Dave Braine said.

I agreed it was pretty big. When you've cracked the Gator Bowl, you've taken a significant step in the college football world. Even though we got hammered, playing Tennessee in the Gator Bowl was big for our fans and big for our whole program. Getting beat like that didn't help, but it was kind of a learning deal.

The Volunteers had Peyton Manning at quarterback and James Stewart at tailback and we lost, 45-23, at the University of Florida's "Swamp." That year the Gator Bowl was being renovated for the new NFL team, the Jacksonville Jaguars. Manning had a big game against us. Between him and Ray Lewis, we got some careers started that year.

That winter Elmassian left to join the staff at Washington, saying he "wanted to compete for the national championship." He didn't think the infrastructure was in place at Tech to do that.

I think the reality of that statement was true at the time. We're getting there. We've increased season ticket sales every year. We're increasing the size of Lane Stadium. Our facilities have gotten better. But look at the schools that have won the national championship over the last decade. Check their stadium size. Check their season ticket sales. We wouldn't be in that same category. In one sense it makes the fact that we played for the national championship in 1999 even more amazing. I understood what he was saying.

I promoted Bud Foster and Rod Sharpless as co-defensive coordinators and hired Lou West from Kent University to fill the open spot.

Although we lost Elmo, we welcomed back Rickey Bustle.

Coach Tranquill had left to join his good friend Nick Saban, who had just been named head coach at Michigan State. It was a loyalty deal. It was also a good thing Billy Hite had kept in touch with Rickey by phone during the season.

"Rickey might come back and join us if you give him a call," Billy said.

I didn't waste much time. I called Rickey and asked him if he would be interested in returning to Blacksburg.

"Yes, I would," he said.

Rickey's main task in the offseason was finding us a starting quarterback. The battle was between redshirt freshman Al Clark and junior Jim Druckenmiller. When Clark suffered a spring practice injury, Druck became the man.

Jim Druckenmiller was a guy who, in practice, you would sometimes say, "geez, he doesn't look very good." But he performed in games.

That's why I think he would have benefited from playing professional football in Europe. He's at his best when he's competing. He just needs to be in a game; he's not as impressive in individual drills. He needs to be evaluated in the heat of competition.

He was a big kid, 6-foot-4, 220, and strong. He won Mike Gentry's offseason Iron Man competition and had a 376-pound hang clean. I always said he was like Jim Kelly. Penn State wanted Kelly as a linebacker, and Druckenmiller could play linebacker. He had that kind of toughness.

Druck's first career start came on Thursday night, September 7, on ESPN against Boston College. He actually played pretty well, passing for 296 yards -- the most ever for a Tech quarterback in his first start. But we had too many dropped passes and converted only three of 16 third downs.

Our next game was against Cincinnati, a team most of our fans expected us to beat. Well, it rained that morning, and for some reason we didn't have our field covered with a tarp. The field turned into a muddy mess. The footing was terrible.

I stood on the sideline before the game, and when I saw those big old Cincinnati guys going through their workouts, I knew we were in trouble. The muddy field took away our big advantage, speed. Cincinnati was bigger than us, and the game became a shoving match.

We had five turnovers in the slippery muck, and Cincinnati converted three of them into scores. The big one was a 71-yard interception return by Brad Jackson. We lost, 16-0.

After the game, senior defensive tackle Jim Baron stood up on a chair in the locker room, covered in mud.

"We will NOT lose another (bleeping) game this season," he said.

It was the most unusual thing I've ever heard a player say in that situation. Here we were, our next game against Miami, a team we had never beaten, and he said we're not going to lose.

The next day, at our Sunday night staff meeting, Billy Hite swore I was going to come in there and fire every one of them. Instead, I said, "There are too many good coaches in this room, and there are too many good players on this team. Let's put them in position to win. Let's go out there this week and coach like we're 2-0."

And I got up and walked out.

That was my thinking. This wasn't the time to panic. I could have flipped out and put all this pressure on my staff, but then everyone would have become tight as a tick.

It worked. And Jim Baron was right.

We went on to win 10 in a row.

20

THE TURNING POINT IN OUR PROGRAM

WHILE THOSE of us on the second floor offices of the Jamerson Athletics Center were calmly preparing for the No. 17 Miami Hurricanes, everybody else was wondering what the heck was happening to our program.

Counting the last part of the 1994 season, we had lost five of our last six games and nearly blew the one win. State rival Virginia hammered us in Blacksburg. Tennessee hammered us in the Gator Bowl. Two coordinators had left to join other schools.

And now we were facing Miami — a team we had never beaten. A team that had hammered us by a combined score of 88-28 the last three seasons.

On top of that we were facing the pass-happy Hurricanes without our best cornerback, Antonio Banks. With Tony out, we had to rely on two true freshmen, Loren Johnson and Pierson Prioleau, to fill the void.

Things were not looking too good.

In the Friday, Sept. 22nd edition of the school newspaper, The Collegiate Times, ran this classified ad: "Lost! Lost! Lost! Hokie football team. Last seen playing in the first half against Rutgers in November of 1994. Big reward if found."

It was time to turn up the wick! So instead of our regular Friday Night Video, I tried something different. After dinner I got everybody in a circle so we could look each other in the eye. Then I called on certain people, guys our team had a lot of respect for. I called on defensive lineman Jim Baron. I called on defensive back William Yarborough. I called on offensive tackle Mike Bianchin. And I called on tailback Dwayne Thomas.

Thomas was normally a quiet guy. But he stood up and looked at his offensive linemen in the eye and said, "If you guys give me just a little crack of space, I'll run that football for you tomorrow."

When I heard that I got chill bumps down my spine.

It was one of the greatest Friday night meetings we ever had. Sometimes you try different motivational things and they don't come out quite right. But I'll tell you now, this one came out right. That was the most together, serious group I've ever walked out of a meeting with on a Friday night. Whew! And the next day those little cracks were big holes and Dwayne rushed for 165 yards.

We beat them, 13-7, but we dominated the game. We blocked a kick and recovered on the six but didn't score. We missed a bunch of field goals and we found out later, watching the video, that our holder was letting go of the ball before it was being kicked.

As it was, the game came down to the last 17 seconds, when Loren Johnson knocked away a pass intended for Yatil Green at the five. Thank goodness the officials didn't throw a flag. When

I went back and looked at the tape I never thought it was an obvious interference. The official could have called it, but it wasn't a bad call not to call it. You get down to the last play like that, it's got to be something obvious.

What a great day. The Virginia Tech Hall of Fame had inducted Bruce Smith the previous night, and he was in the stands for the game. Vaughn Hebron was there, too. When it was over our fans stormed the field and tore down the goalposts.

J.C. Price had nine tackles and four sacks and was named Big East Defensive Player of the Week. He was running down players all over the field. One time he tackled Miami wide receiver Jammi German after a 37-yard catch. That is unheard of.

"I was going to follow them into the bathroom if I had to," he said.

We've had a lot of big moments at Virginia Tech, but beating Miami that day was as big as it's been for us. I'd hate to think what would have happened had we not won that game.

It was the turning point in our program.

That win kicked off an amazing 10-game winning streak. The next Saturday, freshman Angelo Harrison blocked two punts and we beat Pittsburgh, 26-13. Cornell Brown had 13 tackles and we beat Navy, 14-0. Backup quarterback Al Clark had touchdown runs of 48 and 58 yards and we beat Akron, 77-27. Myron Newsome was named National Defensive Player of the Week with 10 tackles, a sack and 71-yard interception for a score and we beat Rutgers, 45-17. Brown had 12 tackles and three sacks and we beat West Virginia, 27-0.

We were 6-2 but still unranked when No. 20 Syracuse came to Blacksburg. ABC was there for the first time since 1981 and the game was hyped as the biggest in Lane Stadium history — at the time. Brown had another big game with nine tackles, three sacks and two forced fumbles and we won, 31-7. The next week we beat Temple, 38-16, at RFK Stadium in Washington, D.C. to clinch our first-ever Big East Championship. There I got another victory shower, this time from Price and Bianchin.

I didn't know if they poured Gatorade or water over me. All I know was that it was wet and it felt good.

Next was No. 13 Virginia, the co-ACC champions, for an ABC-televised game in Charlottesville. The Cavaliers beat No. 2 Florida State that year and had one of their better teams. And they were putting a pretty good whipping on us through three quarters, leading, 29-14.

We cut it to 29-23 and were driving again when they intercepted us with 4:08 left. When a pass interference penalty gave them first down at our 34-yard line with 2:40 to play, I thought the game was over.

Fortunately we still had all three of our timeouts, and we used every one: the first at 2:30, the second at 2:24 and the third at 2:17. We held, and Virginia missed a 47-yard field goal attempt. Now we were back in it, but down by six points with 2:12 left.

And with no timeouts.

Quarterback Jim Druckenmiller's first three passes were incomplete. We faced fourth-and-10 from our own 30, but Druck found Cornelius White across the middle for 14 yards.

Whew!

A couple of passes later Druck had moved us to the Virginia 32.

"Call the Pump and Go," offensive coordinator Rickey Bustle said.

Split end Jermaine Holmes made a quick fake to the inside and Druck pump-faked to him. Virginia's secondary had been aggressive all day and they bit on the fake. Holmes turned upfield. Druck hit him perfectly for the touchdown, Atle Larsen kicked the extra point, and we led, 30-29, with 47 seconds left.

All the Cavaliers needed was a field goal to win, and there was plenty of time remaining. They drove to our 40 with six seconds left, but that would have been a 57-yarder, a little out of their range. Instead they tried a quick sideline pass to get a little closer and stop the clock.

But Antonio Banks stepped up, intercepted the pass and raced 65 yards for a touchdown as time expired. Virginia trainer Joe Gieck got so mad, he sort of stuck out his leg to trip Banks as he ran past him. We won, 36-29, and our fans carried our players off the field, even though the game was in Charlottesville.

We had done it. Jim Baron was right when he stood up there that day, dripping with mud after the Cincinnati game.

There was no secret to our success. It was just dedication and hard work. A blue-collar work ethic.

Before the season, Rod Sharpless, one of my co-defensive coordinators, had brought down this beat-up old rusty black lunch pail from his mother-in-law's house in Mercerville, N.J. It used to belong to a coal-miner. It was missing a latch or two, but it was perfect for us. John Ballein painted an orange-and-maroon "VT" on it and it became a symbol for our defense's blue-collar work ethic.

"Whoever painted that VT on there did a sloppy job of it," linebacker Brandon Semones said.

"That's a workingman's pail," Ballein said. "You think they'd have something painted on there nice and neat?"

The defensive team took that old lunch pail with them everywhere they went: practice, team meetings, the bus, the plane, the hotel, you name it. The top defensive guy each week was responsible for the thing.

Our "Lunch Pail Defense" finished first nationally against the run and fifth nationally in scoring defense. The Big East named me Coach of the Year and Cornell Brown Defensive Player of the Year. Eleven Hokies made conference first or second teams. Our offense scored 321 points -- the second-highest total in school history. We were ranked No. 13 by AP. But since there was no league tie-breaker in place, Miami tied us for the league title.

For a while we thought we would get snubbed for an Alliance bowl, because Miami had the bigger name. But soon after the regular season was over, the NCAA handed down sanctions against Miami. The Hurricanes lost 24 scholarships and were banned from postseason action for 1995.

We were in the Sugar Bowl.

Our fans went crazy, buying up every ticket they could. We sold 12,000 tickets in two days and took an estimated 32,000 fans to New Orleans — even though our ticket allotment was 17,200.

Hokie fans are resourceful, now.

That was such a great trip. One of my lasting memories from it was the phone call I got at the practice field at Tulane from Shayne Graham, telling me he was coming to Virginia Tech. That was big, because Shayne was a heck of a kicker. When you realize you've got that guy for four years, that was a big recruit for us.

Our Sugar Bowl opponent was Texas, which featured all-America defensive end Tony Brackens and the BMW Backfield of quarterback James Brown, tailback Shon Mitchell and future Heisman Trophy winner Ricky Williams.

We didn't play real well early and fell behind, 10-0. Then wide receiver Bryan Still made the play of the game. With 2:34 left in the half, he returned a punt 60 yards for a score. We had a middle return set up, but he got some great blocks from Corney White and Pierson Prioleau, found daylight and broke it down the right side. It was pretty much the same place where Peter Warrick broke his punt against us in 1999.

Still set up our next score with a 27-yard catch to the Texas 2-yard line, and he broke the game open with a 54-yard touchdown catch with 12:28 left. He was named the game's Most Valuable Player.

The longer the game went, the better we got. Our defense turned up the wick, sacking Brown five times and intercepting him three times. Jim Baron capped the scoring by returning a fumble 20 yards for a touchdown and we won, 28-10.

After the game our players jumped into the stands of the Superdome, into the arms of our loyal fans. Cornerback Larry Green carried a big "VT" flag around the field. J.C. Price flexed his biceps and held the lunch pail over his head.

We retired that lunch pail after the game. That summer, John Ballein's mother found a replacement at a flea market in Montana. He painted another "VT" on it and we've used that one ever since.

That was a special group of seniors. Price and Baron were something. They were strong and really fast for their size. That's when we truly realized the advantage of having speed at defensive tackle.

Middle linebacker George DelRicco was such a tough, hard-nosed guy. You KNEW how he was going to play, now. The list goes on: Hank Coleman, Lawrence Lewis, Jeff Holland and William (Killer) Yarborough.

On offense, we had seniors like Still, tailback Dwayne Thomas, wide receiver Jermaine Holmes and offensive linemen Chris Malone and Mike Bianchin.

After that season we lost Rod Sharpless, who became defensive coordinator at Rutgers. He had family ties in New Jersey and the Scarlet Knights were offering him a lot more money. To replace him I interviewed Jim Cavanaugh, who was the receivers coach at North Carolina, and Charley Wiles, who had played for me at Murray State and had been a graduate assistant coach for me at Tech. I told Charley, "I'm going to hire you. I don't know when, but one day I'm going to hire you."

But for this job I hired Jim Cavanaugh

I meant what I said to Charley, though. Not long after that, Todd Grantham took a job with Michigan State, and the same day Charley happened to be in Blacksburg for a coaching clinic. I called him upstairs into my office and said, "Do you want to be the defensive line coach for Virginia Tech?"

"Absolutely," Charley said, and you could just see in his eyes that he was so happy.

It wasn't exactly the same deal when I offered Charley a scholarship to come to Murray State. I don't think he had been recruited a lot, but we flew him up from Florida for the weekend. His father lived in Tennessee and met him on campus. I think they were just kind of hoping for some kind of deal from us: a meal ticket, pay for his books, something like that. It was Sunday morning of his visit, and I brought Charley and his father into my office. We talked about some things then I got down to business.

"We're prepared to offer you a full grant-in-aid," I said.

In a second, Charley's father popped up out of his chair.

"Get up, boy," he said to Charley. "We're going to Murray State!"

As quick as they took the offer, I thought afterward, "aw, geez, I could have gotten that boy for books and a meal plan." But I had made my offer — and I'm glad he came.

WITH MY new staff in place, we looked forward to the 1996 season. We had quarterback Jim Druckenmiller and defensive end Cornell Brown both returning. I knew we were going to be good, but I wasn't prepared for everything that happened.

Although we went 10-1, the regular season was marred with off-field distractions. We had 19 different players charged by the police. In the end, charges were dropped against 10 of the players, and the remaining nine were convicted of misdemeanors. But my thinking is if there is one conviction, that's one too many.

We brought it all on ourselves. It was a fact of life; some guys were in wrong places doing the wrong things. We got a lot of bad publicity for a team that was really pretty good. But our players learned a lot from all of that. They learned to walk away from trouble and they saw what everybody went through, and they didn't want it to happen again.

Our players realize now that if trouble is getting ready to start, they better get away from it.

Some positive things came from it all. The university instituted the Comprehensive Action Plan in place for when someone gets in trouble, and that's good. Now the punishment is up to another person other than the coach. But the best thing was we got some programs in place to help educate our student-athletes. If a guy is educated as to what's right, what's wrong, what is sexual harassment — all these serious issues, then they become responsible for their actions.

So three things came from all those problems in 1996.

No. 1, the kids on our team saw what was happening and never wanted to go through something like that again. No. 2, we implemented our Comprehensive Action Plan. And, No. 3, the punishment was specific, and we did a better job of educating our student-athletes.

As a staff we've always talked about things like this, but since 1996, we've spent even more time. Talking about staying out of trouble, doing what's right, going in the right direction and sometimes just walking away from a situation.

And doing what's right for this football team and doing what's right for yourself. I'm more aware of things that go on around campus now than I was before that particular season. If there is a big spring party planned, I'll always remind the guys to be careful.

The amazing thing was how we played so well through all

the off-field distractions. Our only regular-season loss came at Syracuse.

The best win of the year came at Miami. It was the first time we had ever beaten those old boys at their home, in the Orange Bowl. In fact, it was the first time any team from the Big East had beaten them at home since the league was formed in 1991.

I know they were suffering from scholarship reductions, but they still had great players. And they were still the team to beat in our league. That win was a huge, huge step for our program.

Safety Keion Carpenter, whose career was full of big plays, made his biggest that day. With just 1:54 remaining in the game, Miami trailed by a touchdown and had fourth-and-goal at our eight-yard line. We had discussed whether to stay in zone or go to man-to-man, and we started mixing it up.

I think on that one Miami thought we were in man coverage, but we zoned it. Keion intercepted Scott Covington's pass at the goal line and raced 100 yards for a score. Then Torrian Gray intercepted a pass in the end zone with 40 seconds left to end another Miami scoring threat and we won, 21-7.

We ended the season with back-to-back home wins over our two regional rivals, West Virginia and Virginia, by a combined score of 57-23. Both teams were ranked in the Top 20 at the time.

As Big East champions, the Orange Bowl selected us to play Nebraska on Dec. 31st in Miami. Nebraska! In the Orange Bowl! We were going through new territory here. Ten years ago, it wouldn't have happened.

Nebraska out-gained us by only eight yards (415-407) and we were within three points with less than a minute to play in the third quarter. But the Cornhuskers just physically wore us down and we lost, 41-21.

We played the game a little short-handed, which didn't

help our depth. We lost defensive tackle Nathaniel Williams before the game for disciplinary reasons. And then, once we were in Miami, we sent defensive end Jason Berish home, again for disciplinary reasons. Against a team like Nebraska, you just gotta have them. Let me tell you, we were playing good. We were getting after them, hanging in there for a while. But as the game wore on we became a step slow chasing their quarterback, Scott Frost. What was going for two or three yards in the first half became 10 to 12 yards plays in the second. It was a game where the depth of Nebraska got us. We realized we needed to get a few more players.

The other thing about that game I remembered was how tough Nebraska was. I had never played them before, but I always respected them. Let me tell you, now, after that game I really respected them.

On offense, they don't finesse you. They hammer you. And on defense they attack you. Everything they do, they're beating you up. There's a toughness involved.

If you're playing those guys, you better roll up your sleeves because it's going to be 60 minutes of work. They hammer you with that depth. You've got to have it. You get good competition at a position, plus if someone goes down, you're not in a hole.

That locker room was a sad one. We said goodbye to one of the greatest bunch of seniors we've ever had: Druckenmiller, our offensive leader, and Brown, our defensive leader. Defensive backs Antonio Banks and Torrian Gray, who started in four consecutive bowl games. Defensive tackle Waverly Jackson and linebackers Brandon Semones and Myron Newsome, all smart, aggressive guys.

On offense we lost Corney White, tight end Bryan Jennings and offensive linemen Billy Conaty, T.J. Washington and Jay Hagood.

We finished the year 10-2, ranked No. 13 in the AP and

No. 12 in the USA Today/CNN Coaches poll. We had won 20 of our last 22 games, won two Big East titles and had earned two consecutive Alliance Bowl bids.

We were on quite a roll.

21

A WEEK INSIDE THE HOKIES

WHAT'S A typical week like for me during the season? Come on, I'll show you.

SUNDAY

9 A.M. I sit in with the defensive staff as they grade the film from Saturday's game. Bud Foster runs the projector as each coach grades his player according to a productivity chart. That takes about an hour and a half to two hours.

Then I grade some of the kicking game. I get myself, Danny Pearman, Jim Cavanaugh and Lorenzo Ward together and work on the "Pride" team, which is our punting team. Then I get started grading the "Pride and Joy," or punt block team, and our kickoff coverage team.

12:30 P.M. I look at the video with the offensive staff. They've already done their grading, but I come in and we watch the film together as a staff then.

1:30 P.M. I finish up any other grading that needs to be done. If we had any special issues with officials, I take care of it then. Then I'll go home and take a break for a couple of hours. That sort of separates last week's game from the upcoming game.

6 P.M. I return to the office and begin Pride and Joy, and start studying the opponents' video. Our video staff will have put all of our opponents' punts on one videotape. I'll study that till 9:30, charting punting times, charting punting directions.

There are usually at least three or four games on there, and I'll go through it four or five times. I'll work on a new rush and I'll think of a new return, and then go back and watch the tape to make sure it will work.

9:30 P.M. Staff meeting in the conference room adjacent to my office. This is when we make all the decisions for what I say to the team on Monday afternoon. We have the awards the players make in the dressing room after a game, but now the coaches make their choices.

We choose an offensive player, a defensive player and a special teams player. Then we'll choose the team captains for the next game. Those are always the seniors who played the best on Saturday. We also choose who was the offensive and defensive scout team players of the week, because we want to recognize people for giving good effort. Then we talk about what players have to do punishment. After that, I ask my coaches if there are any special thoughts for the week. Then I send them out of their with my usual thing: "Go man, go!"

10:15 P.M. We go home and get some rest.

MONDAY

7 A.M. Everybody is back in the office. Our players come in to watch the Monday Morning Video, and I finish up my Pride and Joy work, then do kickoff coverage and Pride and get the special teams scouting report done.

11:15 A.M. Sports Information Director Dave Smith comes down and we do the weekly video for the Big East t.v. stations. He will ask me five or six questions and I answer them. Then I tape some quotes for our telephone call-in number. Fans can call in and hear my comments about the game.

11:40 A.M. Big East teleconference.

NOON Racquetball with John Ballein, Rickey Bustle and Bryan Stinespring. We play to 11 — and the first one to 11 wins. Rickey and Bryan always spot me and John five points to keep the game interesting. We used to win about half the time, but not anymore.

I don't really take lunch. I'm not a big lunch guy. I could eat it or not eat it. Sometimes John Ballein's assistant, Bruce Garnes, will bring me back something from the cafeteria, or Diana Clark, my assistant, will bring me a sandwich from this place called Grandma's, and I'll just eat it in the office.

2:30 P.M. Staff meeting. We plan practice. It's already set; we just put it on the board. Then we go over anything else I need to bring up to the team.

3:15 P.M. Team meeting. In front of everybody, I again congratulate those who won the Wes Worsham Player of the

Game award and read off his statistics. Then I'll say, "these players were nominated offensively," and I'll name them. "But the guy the coaches felt was the top offensive player was," and I'll say whoever it was with his statistics.

Then we do it with the defense: who's nominated, who wins the award. Then special teams, and the outstanding guy who wins the Special Forces T-shirt. That's usually the guy who had the most points.

I like recognizing people who play well in front of their teammates. Then I announce who is going to be captains for the next game. Then we announce punishment. These are the people who know they will be running early on Wednesday morning.

We go through our goals chart for offense, defense and special teams. We talk about why we didn't reach certain goals.

Then I show the video of our penalties.

Then, in front of everyone, we show the special teams' Big Hit of the Week, an award we call The Kahuna. That stands for Knock And Hit Until Nobody Answers. I like doing this because it's another way of saying "special teams are important." The offensive and defensive teams will then break up and choose their big hit of the week, but the special teams award is in front of everyone.

Then we break up into offense and defense and go through our scouting report. That goes on for about 45 minutes. Then we have our kicking meetings. We look at video from last week and what we're going to do this week.

5:10 P.M. Practice, full pads. One thing we do on Monday that is a little unusual is our "converge" period. We work on screens, draws, delays, reverses, halfback passes. Unusual plays that are either real good or real bad for either the offense or defense. I like going first team against first team, because it gives us a chance to run these plays against good people.

But I also like it because it's a fast tempo. Whether you won or lost the previous Saturday, it gets you back moving. We're bouncing around there, screaming "here we go," moving around fast. That period starts the week off full speed ahead for the next game.

6:30 P.M. Practice is over. Everybody showers and the team has dinner at what we call Mike Gentry's Training Edge at Dietrick Dining Hall.

7:30 P.M. I come back here and do my radio call-in show with Bill Roth for an hour. Sometimes we do it in here in the football offices, and three or four times during the Fall we do it over at the Volume Two Bookstore.

8:30 P.M. I spend some time watching video of our next opponent until about 10 p.m.

TUESDAY

8 A.M. I'm watching video of our next opponent. Used to be, I'd start every morning with a sausage gravy biscuit from Hardee's, what we call "heart-cloggers." But that didn't go real well. And when things don't go well, I want to stop it.

But each week, a member of the coaching staff will buy breakfast for that week. Who buys depends on who the game means the most to that week. For instance, for Clemson, Danny Pearman or Rickey Bustle will buy breakfast, because they're Tiger alumni. They will give a graduate assistant $25 and he'll head off to Hardee's.

11 A.M. Staff meeting. Before I make any decision regarding our program, we discuss it at these daily meetings. We also talk about what we're going to do at practice. Everybody's in there. Head trainer Mike Goforth is in there and updates us on the injuries. Strength and conditioning coach Mike Gentry is also there, and on Wednesday I check with him to make sure everybody showed up at his Sunrise Service. He tells me what we're going to do conditioning-wise for practice.

Equipment manager Lester Karlin is there in case we have any questions about gear. Kevin Hicks is there for any questions about video. John Ballein is there for everything.

Bruce Garnes sits in there, too. I never make a decision that deals with the overall program unless I get opinions from my people. I'm going to make the final decision, but I want feedback first.

11:30 A.M. I meet with the media at the weekly press conference at the Best Western Red Lion Inn. We do TV and radio first, then have a buffet lunch. Afterward, I address the group, then talk to the writers individually.

2 P.M. I sit down with Dave Smith for anything he might need. That's when I also take care of odds and ends and make any phone calls I need to make.

3:05 P.M. Daily positional meetings for our players. I stay out of those.

4:15 P.M. Practice, full pads. We call Tuesday and Wednesday practices the "work days." Rickey and Bud work on that week's game plan. This also the day we have that middle drill I talked about earlier, going hard against each other 7-on-7.

6:30 P.M. Practice is over. I shower and go home to eat dinner with Cheryl.

8 P.M. I go back to the office and spend time calling

recruits. Then I'll watch the day's video of practice, and more of the opponent if necessary. I do this for about two hours. I never stay later than 10 p.m., and neither does my staff. I don't want them to.

WEDNESDAY

6 A.M. Mike Gentry conducts his Sunrise Service, where he doles out the week's punishment. During the season I won't ask my staff to join Mike, but in the offseason, I'll go some of the time, and the position coach of the player will be there. That kind of reinforces that Mike Gentry doesn't want to be there, and the position coach doesn't want to be there, so we want you to do things right so none of us have to be there. But there always is a trainer present.

We don't conduct Sunrise Service every week, though; it ends up being necessary about half the time.

8 A.M. Next opponent, odds and ends. I used to always meet with the offense and defense at this time, but I don't anymore unless they're something in particular we want to meet about. It's their deal. We have the same philosophy; I'm going to let them work out the details of the game plan. Instead I watch film, answer mail, do all that head coaching odds and ends stuff.

11 A.M. Same meeting as Tuesday.

11:45 A.M. We play racquetball, unless one of our coaches has to speak at the Blacksburg Sports Club.

2 P.M. Meet with Dave Smith regarding media odds and ends. If I have time, I try to get a head start putting together my Friday Night Video.

4:15 P.M. Practice, full pads.

6:30 P.M. Practice is over. I usually try to go home again for dinner. I only live about 10 minutes away so it's easy to do.

8 P.M. Come back to the office, call some recruits and watch some tape of the day's practice. I try not to stay too late on Wednesday. I'm usually home by 9 P.M. at the latest. To relax I'll watch a little TV, whatever's on. I try to stay awake long enough to hear Jay Leno's monologue, but sometimes I don't make it.

THURSDAY

9 A.M. Staff meeting. We decide on our travel squad, go over our weekend itinerary, review our practice schedule and anything else that needs to come up. This will never take more than 45 minutes. Nothing's long here.

9:45 A.M. I finish preparing my Friday Night Video.

11:45 A.M. Racquetball again. I guess I'm a glutton for punishment.

3 P.M. I meet with the kickoff coverage team. This is the only time we ask the kicking team to come in early. We push the positional meetings back to 3:15 p.m. I show a video of last week's game, and we go over what we're going to do this week. I don't want to do that on Monday with the other kicking teams because it seems like it just goes on too long. And we don't work on kickoff coverage until Thursday's practice anyway.

4:15 P.M. Practice, no pads, just sweats. We have a long team period with the offensive and defensive teams going against the scout teams. They work their way down the field, covering all the situations, 1st-and-10, second-and-7, third-and-1 and so forth. That's the day we also practice kickoff return and kickoff coverage. That's the day we'd work on a fake with the punt team.

That's also the day we work on our two-minute drill. It's not so much who wins; it's getting the fundamentals down. Stopping the clock, getting the play called.

5:45 P.M. Practice is over. Thursday's practice is a little shorter. After that, everybody goes home after practice. Most of the coaches usually go out to dinner with the family. All the work is done and there is no reason to come back to the office.

11 P.M. Curfew.

FRIDAY

This day varies, depending on whether we have a home game or away game. If we're on the road, I'll come into the office an hour before we're scheduled to depart. If it's a home game, I might not come in until noon. That's a little window to recharge. I think you need that.

After that 2-8-1 season in 1992, we were in here all hours of the day and we just got run down. And it's not only the hours and not getting sleep, but also the stress of the whole thing. It kind of works against you from both sides.

Another thing that helps us is that most of this staff has been together for so long. We know what each other is doing so we don't have to take a lot of time in meetings. That's one of the reasons this thing works so well. And I have great confidence in Bud Foster and Rickey Bustle to handle their thing. I really believe it's an efficient operation.

That afternoon can vary. If it's a TV game, I'll meet with the broadcast team.

3:05 P.M. Our kicking meetings start.

4:30 P.M. Pregame walk-through in sweats. What we do is stretch, throw the ball around, check special teams situations, break into offense and defense and go over special situations, like running out the clock or the last play of the game. Going over what we do if the punt is blocked. What we do if the ball is past the line of scrimmage. We cover that every week.

For example, with our Pride team, we try to nail a punt inside the 10-yard line. Then we turn it around, putting the ball at the one-yard line and kicking out. We practice kicking at five seconds, we practice against an 11-man rush, which a team will do on the last play of the game. We practice taking a safety with our Pride team. We get the Pride and Joy team and practice blocking kicks. We practice short kicks.

If the opposing punter gets off a short kick, our punt returner is taught to scream, "Peter! Peter! Peter!" then our return team knows to look up, locate the ball and get away from it, so it doesn't land on their head or take a bounce and hit them, letting the other team recover. We use the term "Peter" because it's something you're not supposed to touch!

If it's a home game, we'll catch the bus and go have dinner together at a local restaurant. That's when we'll show the Friday Night Video. If we're on the road, we'll do it at the hotel.

Then if we're home, we see a movie together, chosen by the seniors. Let me tell you there have been several stinkers in there. What worries me is that I'll think it's a terrible movie, and the kids will love it. Makes me wonder if I'm getting out of touch here.

Then we go back to the hotel; even when we're playing at

home, we stay at a hotel in Radford. There we break into our offensive and defensive meetings, going over things for tomorrow's game.

11 P.M. Curfew.

SATURDAY

The itinerary varies depending on game time, but the pregame meal is always four hours before kickoff. If it's a night game, we like to walk just to stretch our legs.

I always meet with my coaching staff the morning of the game to go over anything unusual. Whether we want to run a fake, do we want to make any special substitutions, that kind of thing. Then I meet individually with my coordinators, Bud and Rickey, to discuss strategy and their game plan.

Ten minutes before the departure time, the offense will meet together for the last time, and the defense will meet together for the last time. That's when we give our last motivational speeches.

A lot of people think we meet together before the game and I give this great speech to send our kids running out of the tunnel. Those are not the best motivational times. I've always felt if you have to motivate them that late in the deal, you're going to have a tough time winning the ballgame. You better have taken care of that on Tuesday, Wednesday and Thursday.

When we get to the stadium, everybody dresses, then we go out to warm up. We come back in about 20 minutes before game time and get together in our dressing room. But there's not much said at that point. Everybody is just getting ready to go back out. It's a quiet time. I might make a comment or two, but it's never anything real long.

Then I head out to the field with the team. We take that long walk through that tunnel. And I do love that tunnel. I loved it when I was a player and I love it now. It's one of the great entrances in college football.

John Ballein put that Hokie Stone over the door, and all of our kids touch it before they run out. And man, when you're standing there at the opening, waiting for the introductions, that's one of my favorite moments. Looking over there at that East side, man, it's a big, big side. I love that roar of the crowd when we come running out; it's a great reception. We might change a lot of things in the future at Tech, but I guarantee you we will never change the players' entrance into Lane Stadium.

Then we play the game.

When the game is over, Wes Worsham, one of our university's big contributors, sponsors a party for the coaches and their immediate families. It's a time to relax and enjoy each other after a hard week. We have ESPN on and watch the game recaps and cut loose a little bit and laugh with each other. It's our coaches' time to bust on each other a little bit.

John Ballein jokes that he has to set up a special room for Coach Cavanaugh, with a rocking chair and a blanket. He puts some oatmeal in there and when Coach Cav gets tired he covers him up.

I work hard at putting a staff together who enjoys each other. This is such a tough business, when you have to worry about what you're saying around the office, it makes it a lot tougher. I prefer to have people who like each other and have fun. And this staff is the best we've ever had.

Then, the next morning, it all starts again.

22

DISAPPOINTMENT SET US UP FOR GREATNESS

OUR GOOD fortune continued through the first four games of the 1997 season, when we outscored our opponents by a combined 163-35. Now we had won 24 of our last 26 going into a sun-washed Lane Stadium for Homecoming against Miami of Ohio.

Ironically, the Redhawks beat us at our own game. We had two punts blocked, lost two fumbles and gave up a 32-yard touchdown on a fake field goal and lost, 24-17. From that point on we struggled, losing four of our next seven. We beat Miami for the third year in a row, then dropped our last three, including a 42-3 setback to North Carolina in the Gator Bowl.

We finished a disappointing 7-5 and gave up a lot of big scoring plays. It wasn't like us. We had a lot of new faces for 1998, so I was concerned. After the season my staff collected all those long plays we gave up in 1997 and put them on a video tape. We wanted to show our players it wasn't our scheme that was the problem. It was making the play. It was a matter of bearing down.

That offseason we lost two assistants. Offensive line coach J.B. Grimes accepted an offer from Texas A&M, and that summer Terry Strock agreed to take over the athletic department's Monogram Club.

To fill the spot left by J.B., I hired Tony Ball, who had been receivers coach at Louisville. I had never met him and didn't know what he looked like. That spring I took a return flight to Roanoke, and as I went to my seat I saw a sharp-dressed guy sitting a few aisles in front of me. When we landed at Roanoke, Rickey Bustle was there. I wasn't expecting him. Then I realized he wasn't there for me. He was shaking hands with the sharp-dressed guy.

You guessed it. It was Tony Ball.

Tony is a very dapper dresser and keeps himself in good shape. He has this rule that he does not eat after 8 p.m., which is fine, but that caused a minor problem one year at an annual coaching retreat.

I started doing this in 1993. Before freshmen report in August, I get my staff together at Groundhog Mountain. We play golf and go over the playbook. We've been to a bowl every year we've done it, so even though other resorts have called and invited us, we've always gone to Groundhog.

The offensive staff always arrives a day early, plays golf, meets with me and has dinner, then the next day the defensive staff arrives and we have a coaches' golf tournament. Then the offensive staff leaves and the defensive staff meets with me the next day.

Tony got out there with us that first day and was hitting the ball sideways. He was losing balls all over the course, in the woods, in the water, everywhere. He had a tough day. Dinner was scheduled for 9 p.m., but he has that rule about not eating after 8 p.m. The next morning he drove back to Blacksburg, missing our coaches' golf tournament. Several of our arriving defensive coaches saw him on the way out.

Later that morning, John Ballein is getting the coaches' golf tournament together.

"Where's Tony?" he said.

"We saw him driving home this morning," Charley Wiles said.

That left the tournament short a player, since Jim Cavanaugh and Billy Hite don't play golf. Let me tell you, our staff still gives Tony grief about that one.

Another one of my assistants, Danny Pearman, was fired from Alabama late in 1997.

Now it was the spring of 1998 and Danny couldn't find work anywhere. He sent his application to every Division I-A coach in the country. All coaches have a standard reply form for this, because they receive so many inquiries. But I made sure I added a hand-written note at the bottom, thanking him for his interest, and if anything ever opened up, I would contact him.

Hey, I applied for a lot of jobs when I was an assistant, too. I knew what it was like. Back then I promised myself that if I ever became a head coach, I would respond to any inquiry personally.

Well one Friday night that spring, at about 10 p.m., I called him. He was packing to go to the beach early the next morning for a family vacation. When Danny answered the phone, he thought it was an Alabama GA playing a trick on him, kicking him while he's down.

I explained that I had an opening on my staff. "Well, look, coach, I have to take my family to the beach in the morning," he said. "But once I get them there, I can meet you anytime, anyplace, anywhere. I'll drive; you don't have to worry about flying me anywhere." He left me his cell phone number and I called him Monday morning.

We exchanged small talk and I said something about meeting up in Blacksburg. Then I said, "Danny, wait a minute. Where are you?"

"Coach, I'm at Hilton Head, South Carolina."

I said, "Son of a gun, that's where I am. The heck with going back to Blacksburg. Do you play golf?"

He said, "Coach, well, I'm a hacker, but I can get out there and play."

So that Wednesday we brought Bryan Stinespring and Rickey Bustle down and the four of us got together for a round. "Danny, you and Rickey ride together and get to know each other," I said.

We played 18 holes, and when Danny wasn't around, I went up to Rickey and Bryan.

"Do you like him?" I asked.

"Yeah," they said.

When we had finished, Bryan and I won four dollars from them. Danny had his head down, and as they were riding up to the clubhouse, he turned to Rickey and said, "I've been out of work almost four months. I left my family on vacation to come over here. I hardly have a dime to my name. Surely Coach Beamer isn't going to ask for my four dollars."

Rickey turned to him and said, "I'll tell you what. You better come up with that four dollars."

He was right. I had my hand out for that four dollars before I offered him the job.

A week before our opening game of the 1998 season, our staff suffered a shocking loss. Longtime trainer Eddie Ferrell passed away.

Eddie was a special guy and it was a terrible loss when he died. Everybody loved him so much. He could say the darndest things. If anybody else said them you'd want to punch them out, but Eddie could get away with it. I remember my first year here, 1987, we were having an awful time scoring points. It was a home game and there was a terrible accident where a student fell from the stands.

"You didn't hear about it?" Eddie said.

"No," I said. "What happened?"

"Well, you finally got a first down and a student up in the stands was so surprised, she passed out from shock and fell out of the stadium."

He would always laugh right after getting you. That was his cue that he was just having fun.

One year we were playing up in Boston. We scheduled an early walk-through to beat the traffic and decided to order chicken for our players. "I'll take care of it," Eddie told John Ballein.

On the way back to the hotel after the workout, John leaned over to Eddie. "Don't forget about the chicken," he said, and Eddie got on his cell phone to check on the order.

"I need to speak to the manager," Eddie said. He listened. "He's not there? Well, he's supposed to be. We've ordered 120 boxes of chicken."

There appeared to be a problem and Eddie didn't want me to know about it, so he got up out of his seat and walked toward the back of the bus. I kinda looked back at him. Eddie was getting agitated, pacing up and down the aisle. Finally he yelled, "I don't CARE! I just don't CARE!" and hung up.

He returned to his seat and John leaned over to him.

"You order the chicken?" he said.

"Yeah," Eddie said. "It's not ready yet."

"Then what don't you care about?" John said.

"They need to cook 360 pieces of chicken in less than an hour," Eddie said, "and the guy asked me if we wanted 'regular' or 'extra crispy.' "

Eddie was something. He had one of those little fertilizer

spreaders that worked off the wheels. He poured the fertilizer in there and started walking and realized it was coming out too fast. So he sped up, and the fertilizer came out even faster. He began running, but that spun the wheels that much faster. The faster he went, the more the fertilizer poured out.

The players just loved him. They wore "EF" stickers on the backs of their helmets to honor him and chanted his name after every win that season.

Heck, everybody loved him.

That 1998 season was such an emotional year. It just ripped your heart out. We went 9-3 but were three plays from a perfect season.

After every single loss we came back and won the next one. A lot of teams can't do that. That showed me our kids have a lot of fight in them.

We lost our top two quarterbacks to injuries that year and were forced to move our free safety, Nicky Sorensen, to quarterback. We had discussed playing freshman Michael Vick, but we had promised Tommy Reamon, his high school coach, that we would redshirt him.

Sure, Michael would have come in and made plays, but he needed more time to learn. Sometimes when you play a kid before he's ready, he gets into a bad situation and the next time he starts to think about it. It's like in golf on a tight hole and you knock it in the water. You've had a negative experience there, and the next time you're in that situation, who knows? So yes, we discussed it, but it was never an issue. We had given Coach Reamon our word and that was that.

Although our offense struggled the whole year, it seemed like our defense and special teams would always find a way to score. We blocked 12 kicks and our defense and special teams scored nine touchdowns. Sixteen different players scored touchdowns for us that season.

Defensive end Corey Moore really turned up the wick that

season. Here was a guy, 5-foot-11, 212 pounds, who came off that corner like a rocket. He really changed the game. I've always believed in speed being more important than size, and Corey confirmed that issue. It also confirmed that our strength and conditioning program works. For a guy not very tall, he didn't get knocked around. He was the one knocking people around.

Our three losses that year were gut-wrenchers. We lost to Temple, 28-24, when we dropped a touchdown pass in the final 30 seconds. We lost to Syracuse, 28-26, when Donovan McNabb found tight end Stephen Brominski for a 13-yard scoring pass as time expired. And we lost to Virginia, 36-32, after leading, 29-7, at halftime.

That Syracuse game was a tough one. McNabb had thrown up on the field right before he threw that touchdown pass. I mean he was dying out there. We called timeout to make sure our kids knew what was coming, and we had told them to watch for that exact play. We just didn't execute.

You talk about an emotional game. That was one of the saddest locker rooms I've ever been in. I wanted to say something that would help. I'm not sure what I said did any good, but I just wanted to get the point across that we need to all help each other get through it. We're not going to blame this guy or that. Effort wasn't the issue in that ballgame.

Then there was that Virginia game. We had them beat and let it get away.

Now, I will only make one comment in this book about officials, and this is it.

It was early in the fourth quarter and we were driving to the end zone, and we had just busted it up the middle down to about the Virginia 4-yard line. I looked out on the field and there was a yellow flag. One of the ACC officials called holding back at the line of scrimmage.

After the game I looked at the tape, and looked, and

looked, and looked for that holding call, and I never found it. I sent the tape in for review and never got much of a response. It seemed like I cared a whole lot more about that call than they did.

After the game I met with Clemson officials in Mt. Airy, N.C., about the Tigers' head coaching opportunity. Clemson president Deno Curris had hired me at Murray State in 1981, and I had good memories of the state of South Carolina from my days at The Citadel. Meeting with them helped get my mind off the Virginia loss. A week later, South Carolina athletic director Mike McGee visited my house in Blacksburg and we talked about the Gamecocks' head coaching job.

I was involved in both situations but neither school offered me the job. I felt obligated to check out those opportunities, but I had no real desire to leave Virginia Tech. I liked what was happening here.

With that behind me, my staff and I prepared for the inaugural Music City Bowl in Nashville to play Alabama.

I was glad to play a team like Alabama. You look at some of the programs we've faced in bowl games: Texas, Tennessee, Alabama, Florida State. These are programs with great tradition. One day I hope people will consider Virginia Tech in that same way. And the way you get that is by playing those schools and beating them.

I don't know if we could have had a better setting for that game. People might laugh when I say that because the weather was so cold and wet. But to me, other than the wind, and maybe a heavy snow, I don't think weather is ever a big factor — as long as you have that tarp covering the field.

We won, 38-7, and after the game, Alabama coach Mike Dubose said, "We want to get to the point where Virginia Tech is." I think he realized he had played a pretty good team.

We had quite an Alabama connection going that year. I had hired Danny Pearman, who was an ex-Alabama assistant. We played the Crimson Tide in the Music City Bowl. Then, after the season, I hired a former Alabama defensive back, Lorenzo Ward, who had been coaching at Tennessee-Chattanooga. He replaced defensive backs coach Lou West, who accepted an offer from Notre Dame.

Ward played for the Tide from 1986-90. His teammates had nicknamed him "Whammy" because of his fierce hits. In one of our first interviews, I brought him into my office and I told him, "I want you to understand that there are three head coaches on this staff. There's me. Then there's the head coach of the offense, Rickey Bustle, and there's the head coach of the defense, Bud Foster. Since you are a defensive coach, the final decision to hire you will rest with Bud, but what I want to see is camaraderie. If I see there's camaraderie, that will be my OK, but Bud will make the final decision."

Bud took him in a meeting room and asked Whammy about some techniques. I stopped by and listened in. The thing with Whammy, now, is that he talks very fast. So he started going on explaining some techniques, and I looked at Bud thinking, "What the heck did he just say?"

After the interview was over I talked to Bud in the hallway. "Bud," I said, "Whammy talks awfully fast. Do you think the kids will be able to understand what he's saying?"

"Oh yeah," Bud said. "I just think he was a little nervous."

Whammy hadn't been here long when he learned about one of my pet peeves. It was right after spring practice and we were in a staff meeting. Now, I don't like guys chewing tobacco. I have a rule that if you're chewing tobacco, don't leave your spit cup around, or tape it up. We were discussing personnel, and I asked Whammy about a player. He started answering and in mid-sentence he stopped to spit into a paper cup.

Every coach in that room stopped what they were doing. John Ballein had a look on his face as if to say, "uh-oh."

I gave Whammy a look then turned to Charley Wiles and

Rickey Bustle, who also chew.

"Look, you guys better get him straightened out," I said.

We got Whammy straightened out just fine. Then we survived a scare when Florida head coach Steve Spurrier offered our defensive coordinator, Bud Foster, the same job for the Gators. I know it was a compelling offer for Bud, but he decided to stay at Virginia Tech.

I think he knew we were going to be good.

23

GO MAN,
GO

IT WAS LATE June 1999, and my family and I were
vacationing at our lake house outside Atlanta. We rode into
town to do some shopping and now we were heading back to
the lake house, on Peachtree Street. Cheryl and Casey were in
the back seat, and Shane was in the front seat, reading one of
the preseason football magazines.

Now, I don't usually read the preseason football magazines
unless I think they're going to say something good about us.

I was kind of looking at a few that summer.

This magazine predicted us to do pretty well, and we started talking about our chances.

"You guys take a look at our schedule," I said. "If Michael
Vick plays well for us, tell me what teams have better than a 40
percent chance of beating us."

Cheryl, Casey and Shane each studied the schedule.

"I don't see one," Shane said.

"I don't, either," said Cheryl. Casey agreed.

"You know," I said, "I think you guys are right."

GAME ONE
No. 11 Hokies 47, James Madison 0
September 4, Blacksburg

We didn't want any "Temples" this year, so we referred to each opponent by the game number. That way every game held the same importance. Our deal was, we weren't trying to go 11-0. We were trying to go 1-0 eleven times. John Ballein made up a bunch of signs that he hung on the fence around our practice field: "Prepare To Win No. 1." After each game, he would update the number. The point was that the opponent didn't matter. What was important was winning each game.

We had dedicated this game to two families who had suffered heartbreaking losses.

Marques Hampton, a great young man who had agreed to play for us, died in a car accident along with his mother on his way back home from a campus visit. And Jay and Shelly Poole were big Hokie fans who lost their teenage son, Tom. The Pooles wrote a letter that just tore your heart out, telling us how much they loved our football team.

We don't give out game balls unless we win, so I told our guys, "we have to win this game, because we have two families we want to remember today. We want to give them game balls."

Fans will always remember this game as Michael Vick's debut. We had seen him in practice and knew he was going to be good. The thing that sets him apart is his release; it's just so quick.

But I don't think we realized just how good he was going to

be. So much of his game is elusiveness, and in practice, we're blowing the whistle before he gets hit. Or our defenders were told just to wrap him up instead of tackling him. He's a guy you can't fully appreciate unless he's going full speed.

In less than a half against James Madison he had completed 4 of 6 passes for 110 yards and scored three times. But what everybody remembers is The Flip.

Late in the first half we were on the seven-yard line and Michael scrambled to his right, saw an opening and leaped toward the end zone. While he was airborne a JMU player hit him. Michael did a somersault and his ankles bucked beneath him as he landed.

I got a sick feeling. I thought he was hurt bad. I thought he was done. I remember sliding over to see our team physician, Dr. Duane Lagan, who examined him.

"What do you think?" I said.

"It could go either way," he said.

That wasn't making me feel any better.

"When he went down, I might as well have been talking to air," Bryan Stinespring later explained. "Everybody was looking at Michael. Our kids, 27 cameras on the sidelines, 50,000 fans."

Michael suffered a lower leg contusion and missed the rest of the game, but we won, 47-0. We all piled in our locker room under the stands of Lane Stadium, and it was truly an emotional moment. The giving of the game balls has evolved into a very special thing with our football team; like the Friday Night Video, it's something nobody connected with our team wants to miss.

I love it because we will have an offensive player standing up on a chair and giving a game ball to a defensive player, and vice versa. They're saying how they feel about each other. There are lots of unselfish acts and it is a great morale booster. And nearly every time a player has a tough game and comes back to play well, one of his teammates will reward him with a game ball. You can bank on it.

But this time we didn't give any players game balls.

They went to Jay and Shelly Poole and Andre Hampton, brother of Marques.

GAME TWO
No. 11 Hokies 31, Alabama-Birmingham 10
September 11, Blacksburg

Before the game, I got in front of the team and said, "How many of you think we're a Top 10 team? Show your hands."

Everybody raised them.

"Then either we will play like one and be in the Top 10," I said, "or we won't, and we'll be around No. 30."

Although Michael was out, we really didn't alter our offensive game plan. We didn't run quite as much option, but that was all. Dave Meyer did a fine job of filling in. I think if he ever played a lot, he'd be a very good quarterback. He completed 12 of 21 passes for 144 yards and we won Game Two.

GAME THREE
No. 8 Hokies 31, Clemson 11
September 23, Blacksburg

We had the following weekend off, which gave Michael's leg more time to heal for our Thursday night ESPN matchup with Clemson.

Before the game I told our kids, "When things get big, think small. The next play is what you can control."

Michael threw three interceptions, but the big story was Corey Moore, who had his national coming-out party. He had two sacks, three tackles behind the line of scrimmage, forced a fumble and returned it for the game-clinching touchdown.

Corey won the game ball and gave it to Coach Hite to give to his wife, Anne, who had been ill.

GAME FOUR
No. 8 Hokies 31, No. 24 Virginia 7
October 2, Charlottesville

Our Monday staff meeting was a little longer than usual. I went over all of Virginia's positions, and I could tell my coaches were tense. There was no joking around; we all knew this was a big game. Virginia had beaten us two consecutive years. If anything, playing the Cavaliers is bigger now that ever. Both teams are good, and we're each playing for the pride of our respective conferences. You're talking about two teams somewhere in the national picture with state pride and conference pride on the line. It's bigger now more than ever.

I broke up my meeting with my usual "Go man, go." Everybody split but Whammy, who sat there a moment longer.

"Damn," he said, "there were some tight rear ends in here."

Things loosened up during our Friday Night Video session. Those things are so popular our administrators plan their day around it. President Torgersen never misses one. We have a lot of fun with them, and my coaches aren't immune. One year defensive line Coach Charley Wiles hurt his ankle, couldn't exercise and gained a few pounds, and he's a big guy to begin with. So we showed video of him on the sidelines, from behind, struggling to bend down and pick something up.

"Hey, look!" somebody said. "Charley found something to eat!"

Understand we have a very close-knit staff. And you have to be able to take a lot of good-natured ribbing.

But most of the videos feature our players. For instance,

after the Clemson game, I showed a great hit linebacker Jamel Smith put on Tiger receiver Brian Wofford over the middle. Remember that Jamel grew up in South Carolina wanting to play for Clemson.

Jamel had this high-pitched voice, and tailback Shryone Stith did a great imitation of him. When I showed Jamel's hit I yelled out, "Shyrone! What do you think Jamel is thinking about that time?"

In that high-pitched voice, Shyrone said, "You didn't want me, but they like me at Virginia Tech!" The kids just cracked up.

Right before the Virginia game I told our players to forget about last week. "It's time to turn up the wick!" I said.

Less than six minutes into the game, Michael hit Andre Davis on a beautiful 60-yard bomb for the game's first score. I don't think that play could have been any better. Michael made a great, long throw to a fast receiver on the dead run. And it was to a guy, Davis, whom we really wanted to get going. He's a tall kid who can really run.

We led, 31-7, going into the fourth quarter and people later asked me why I didn't take the first team out sooner. But I had flashbacks to the year before, when Virginia came back from a 29-7 halftime deficit to beat us. I just wanted to get first downs and see the clock run.

This year the game was ours. I don't know if beating Virginia makes a difference in recruiting, because the personality of the two schools is so different. This year, though, a couple of the kids we signed said it made a difference.

GAME FIVE
No. 5 Hokies 58, Rutgers 20
October 9, East Brunswick, N.J.

After our regular Friday afternoon walk-through at the stadium, we boarded our buses to ride back to our hotel, which was only three and a half miles away. We had a police escort. So off we went, and I was thinking about tomorrow's game, not really watching, but the ride back seemed to take longer than it should. Finally we got off an exit, and I saw a sign that said, "Welcome to Rutgers Stadium." We had gone around in a big circle! One hour and 50 miles later, with a police escort, mind you, we finally returned to our hotel. That was just an omen of what was to come.

It was a 6 p.m. start of the game, so we knew we would be arriving in Blacksburg late. Moreover, we usually landed in Roanoke and bussed home, but the Roanoke airport had construction so we were going to land in Lynchburg, about an hour further away. My plan was to send my assistant coaches home on a smaller plane so they could get some rest, and I would stay with the team.

Well, our charter flight had another team on its itinerary and was running late. Then we learned we had to land in Greensboro because Lynchburg was fogged in. By the time we get to Greensboro it was about 3 a.m.

"I tell you want I'm going to do," defensive end John Engelberger said to John Ballein on the bus to Blacksburg. "I'm going to beat up the bus driver so I can get arrested. That way I will go to jail and have a warm bed to sleep in."

At about 4:30 a.m. our bus broke down in Roanoke. As we pulled over on the side of the road I turned to John Ballein.

"Perfect," I said. "Absolutely perfect."

We finally got home at 5:30 a.m.

That story reminds me of another charter flying adventure

from a few years ago on a trip to Greenville, N.C., to play East Carolina. It was with an airline our coaches simply referred to as "Air Guadalupe."

This was when the athletic department was still financially strapped, and I got the feeling it was trying to save some money with this airline. As we were standing on the tarmac at the Roanoke airport I went up to assistant athletic director Jeff Bourne and said, "do you feel good about this deal?"

"I feel real good about this deal," Jeff said.

"Sounds to me like we're cutting corners," I said.

"No, it's going to be fine," Jeff said.

All of a sudden this bright lime green thing came out of the air.

One of our players said, "Look! There's our plane!"

Another one said, "Hey! It looks like a giant pickle!"

I was standing next to Jeff, and his face turned bright red.

We all piled into the plane and got settled in. It was about 90 degrees inside and we were starting to sweat. Then the pilot got on the intercom.

"We have a mechanical problem," he said. "But we brought our maintenance worker, Jose, with us, and he is going to try to fix it."

John Ballein turned to me and said, "they've got a maintenance worker?"

Right about then this fellow wearing overalls ran down the aisle carrying a little screwdriver and a wrench.

I turned to John. "He's going to fix this big plane with THAT?"

We sat on the plane for at least an hour and I asked John to check to see what was going on. He went up front and returned a few minutes later.

"Coach, there's good news and bad news."

"Aw, geez," I said. "Give me the good news first."

"The good news is Jose says the plane is fixed and we're

ready to take off."

"That is good. What's the bad news?"

"Jose is out on the tarmac waving goodbye. He refuses to get back on the plane."

Although we arrived safely, the airline must have known we were a little wary, because the next week we had a brand new white plane. It looked gorgeous. We boarded and sat down; we always had the same seat assignments for every road trip. Eddie Ferrell and Billy Hite sat next to each other up near the front, and Eddie started looking around.

"You know what," he said, "this is the same damn plane we had last week."

"Yeah, right," Billy said. "If it's the same plane, then there should still be a plastic fork I stuck down here in this tray bin."

He opened the tray bin and sure enough, there was a plastic fork.

GAME SIX
No. 4 Hokies 62, No. 16 Syracuse 0
October 16, Blacksburg

We were rising up the national polls and now ESPN's *Gameday* was in town for the first time. That crew of Chris Fowler, Lee Corso and Kirk Herbstreit only travels to college football's hot spots each week to host that Saturday's televised football action, so it said a lot about our program when they decided to come to Blacksburg.

Herbstreit came out to our Friday walk-through and threw some passes to our backs. That was fine with me because, being an ex-Big Ten quarterback, he sure threw the ball a heck of a lot better than Billy Hite.

That Friday I met with the ESPN folks and talked about the game. I told them some stuff about our team that I wouldn't want the other team to know, but I trusted them. I don't think they could play both sides of the fence and last long in this business.

The crowd was at a fever pitch. Before the game, I told our players, "These are special times. There are a lot of distractions, with *Gameday*, Homecoming and national TV, but we need to concentrate on the next play. That is what you can control."

I fully expected that game to be decided late in the fourth quarter, but this time WE would win it on the last play of the game instead of them.

We got an early break and things snowballed from there. Anthony Midget wrapped up wide receiver Quinton Spotwood and punched the ball away, and Cory Bird picked it up before it hit the ground and ran 26 yards for a score. One good thing happened after another and the momentum kept building.

We won, 62-0, and from then on people perceived us in a different light. Here was Syracuse, a legitimate nationally-ranked team that some people had picked to win the game. For us to beat them by such a large margin turned some heads. It made a definite impression on the national media.

GAME SEVEN
No. 3 Hokies 30, Pittsburgh 17
October 30, Pittsburgh, Pa.

Maybe we got to feeling a little overconfident after that big win, because this gameday we had players late for meetings. We even had two coaches miss a meeting. Before boarding the bus for the game, I told everybody, "you had better get it right between here and the stadium — because you don't have it right. Let's go."

Although we won the game, Pittsburgh quarterback David Priestley, a sophomore transfer from Ohio State, passed for 407 yards. Receiver Antonio Bryant had 215 yards receiving against us.

Whammy was one of the guys who had missed our staff meeting, and now his secondary had given up 400 yards passing. After the game Whammy was in the locker room getting dressed when Charley Wiles walked up to him.

"Coach wants to see you," Charley said.

Whammy got a concerned look on his face. "Uh, what about?" he said.

"He says (Pittsburgh head coach) Walt Harris is waiting for you outside," Charley said. "He wants to buy you a damn beer."

After all the problems we had traveling home from Rutgers, we asked the seniors if they wanted to come back Saturday night — and risk another late arrival — or stay overnight in Pittsburgh.

It was a close vote, but we decided to let the players stay overnight and get a good rest. The coaches had to get back to Blacksburg to begin grading film and prepare for West Virginia, so we flew back on a smaller plane while John Ballein stayed with the team.

"How many miles is it from here to Blacksburg?" Whammy asked as we boarded the plane.

"About 500 miles," said the attendant.

"Damn, Whammy," graduate assistant Billy Houseright said. "That's about what Pittsburgh threw on us tonight."

After the regular season we were in a staff meeting, mulling over nominations for the All Big-East team.

"I think we should nominate that Pitt quarterback," Whammy said. "He was pretty good."

"I guess you WOULD think he was pretty good," I said.

It should be said we were played most of that second half with a depleted secondary. Anthony Midget suffered a groin injury and Ike Charlton got poked in the eye, both in the second quarter. Redshirt sophomore Larry Austin and redshirt freshman Ronyell Whitaker replaced them.

I really respect those two guys because they took a lot of heat but they never backed down. Both practiced hard after that game and got better, and both played well from then on out.

When the players all arrived in Blacksburg the next day, we were minus senior linebacker Jamel Smith. He had missed the plane. We were all very worried about him because we didn't know where he was. We even called his mother. Turns out he had stayed overnight with a friend. We tracked him down and he rode home with Coach Cavanaugh's wife, Marsha, who had driven to the game.

GAME EIGHT
No. 3 Hokies 22, West Virginia 20
November 6, Morgantown, WVa.

Sometimes when things are going good, you need to change the pace to keep everybody focused. So instead of our Friday Night Video, I asked some players and coaches to say a few words to our team. It was just time to do something different.

Senior defensive tackle Nathaniel Williams said a few words. Then Shyrone Stith, Coach Cav, Billy Hite and graduate assistant Chris Malone. Nobody talked for more than a minute; some were even shorter.

Then I asked Whammy to say a few words: "Gentlemen, let me tell you this," he began. He started talking in that fast manner of his, pacing across the room. He was talking from the heart. He stopped and we thought he was finished. Then he spun around, pointed, and said, "and GENTLEMEN ..." and went on again, like a preacher, for another five minutes, which seemed like an eternity compared to the other guys.

If we were going to win this game, we were going to be

inspired by the emotional words of the Reverend Lorenzo Ward.

All week there had been a lot of talk about the Bowl Championship Series computer rankings. My stand was simple: the two best teams would play for the national title.

I told our players not to get sucked into BCS conjecture. Don't get dragged into a conversation about it because if you do you'll just talk all day and get nothing solved. We made a conscious effort to just win the next game and let the media worry about the other stuff.

It was out of our control. But things started to fall our way that afternoon. During pregame warmups we learned that Minnesota had upset No. 2 Penn State, 24-23, with a last-second field goal.

"That doesn't mean (squat)," Corey Moore said. "We've got to take care of business."

I don't think the news had an effect on the team. We outgained West Virginia, 469-299, and led, 19-7, with just 4:59 remaining. Then crazy things started happening.

WVU fumbled the ensuing kickoff, but Boo Sensabaugh picked it up and raced 44 yards. We hit him out of bounds, which tacked on another 15 yards, and suddenly WVU was at our 24. I'm thinking, "aw, geez." The Mountaineers scored four plays later, and I began to wonder if things weren't meant to be.

We got the ball and tried to run out the clock. Shyrone Stith fumbled, and, you know, Shyrone hardly ever fumbled. Now WVU had the ball at our 32 and I was going, "aw, geez." Backup Mountaineer quarterback Brad Lewis threw his second touchdown pass and we trailed, 20-19, with 1:15 to play.

I looked over at Michael Vick, and everything was under control. There was no panic. To him it looked like there was plenty of time. He seemed like he was really looking forward to getting back in there.

We started at our own 15 with no timeouts, and I went to

Michael and said, "If we can just get the ball to their 40, we can win." It would be a 57-yard field goal, but Shayne Graham would have a chance.

First, Michael hit Terrell Parham for fourteen yards. Then he found Andre Davis for nine.

Next came the most unbelievable play I've ever seen. Michael scrambled out of the pocket and had gotten enough for the first down. He was running right at me and I thought he was going to go out of bounds. But then, woosh, he went right by me. That might be the fastest I've ever seen a human run. He went 26 yards to the WVU 36 with 23 seconds left.

It would have been a long one, but we were in Shayne's range.

Michael found Hall again for nine yards to the 27. He spiked the ball to kill the clock with five seconds left. It was a 44-yard field goal. From this point on, it was up to placekicker Shayne Graham.

Now, I have this policy that nobody talks to the kickers. But assistant coach Danny Pearman didn't know this rule when he first joined us in 1998. It was during spring drills; he was watching film of the kickers and noticed every time Shayne kicked the ball, he swung around his arm to keep his balance. Danny began making fun of Shayne in the back of the room, making a winding motion with his hands.

Later that day Shayne visited John Ballein's office and said, "Coach Pearman really helped me with my kicking today."

"Wait a minute," John said. "You're telling me one of our coaches talked to you about your kicking?"

"Yes. Coach Pearman. He was very helpful."

"Hold on," John said. "I have to get this on tape."

John pulled out his mini-cassette recorder and asked Shayne to repeat the story. Then he came into my office.

"Danny talked to the kickers today," John said.

"Which one?" I said.

"Shayne Graham," he said. "Listen to this." And he played me the tape.

"Let me have the tape," I said.

That night we had a staff meeting and I asked Coach Billy Hite, "Billy, what is my rule with the kickers?"

Billy said firmly, "NEVER TALK TO THE KICKERS."

Then I took out John's tape recorder and hit "play."

There was John Ballein's voice saying, "Shayne, what happened to you today?"

Next was Shayne's voice. "Well, I was kicking the other day and wasn't doing very well. Coach Pearman watched the film and pointed out that I was moving my arm in the wrong direction. I told him, 'That was very helpful, coach. I never really thought about it until just now.'"

Danny was just sitting there with his head down going, "oh, no." But he learned that rule.

Now you know why nobody said anything to Shayne Graham before he tried that kick. There was nothing that I could tell him at this point that he didn't already know. To talk to him at that point would have been a distraction.

Instead, all I said was a little prayer.

Then, right as he lined up to kick, a little wind came up. I thought, "aw, geez. This is just what we need."

But Shayne knocked the ball right down the middle. From the sidelines, it is often difficult to tell if a ball goes through the goalposts or not, so I watched it closely. I didn't react until I saw the officials put up their hands.

People said my security officer, Jody Falls, had to hold me up after that kick. But I'm not sure I wasn't holding Jody up. Geez, what a game. I felt bad for WVU head coach Don Nehlen, because we've all been through those kinds of heart-breakers. But it was a great win for us.

Our national title hopes were still alive.

That locker room was something after that game. It was

one of the neatest times you could ever have. Cheryl came in and I don't know if she's ever done that before. A lot of times, she asked me what I said or what happened in there. But she was there to see that one.

To go undefeated, you probably have to experience a game like that. Going undefeated is so hard to do in college football. So many teams can beat each other. But after we got that one, I started to think maybe this was going to be our year.

Why? In that game, we had two key people come through for us: The quarterback and the kicker. If you're going to go all the way, those two guys have to perform every time, all the time.

GAME NINE
No. 2 Hokies 43, No. 19 Miami 10
November 13, Blacksburg

Although we had no Friday Night Video last week, Jamel Smith wasn't going to get off the hook for missing the plane that easily. John Ballein had remembered a recruiting video we had done several years ago that showed our plane taking off into the sunset. He dug that up and we spliced into the video. After that we spliced in a tape of Jamel.

"Shyrone!" I said. "What is Jamel saying here?"

Shyrone Stith did his high-pitched voice again. "I'm here! I'm here!" he said. "Don't leave me! Don't leave me!"

Before the season, the Hurricanes had marked this game on their calendar. We had beaten them four years in a row and they were really gunning for us. Since we were coming off such an emotionally draining game at West Virginia, I was worried.

ESPN's *Gameday* returned to Blacksburg for this one, and that said a lot, because they rarely go back to the same place twice in one season. It was a real tribute to our fans and our

Lane Stadium/campus setting.

This was the most-hyped game in Big East Conference history. In addition to Gameday, writers from the New York, Chicago, Boston and San Diego dailies were there, plus Sports Illustrated.

The game was plenty big enough, but it got bigger just before kickoff. That's when we learned that the No. 2 team in the BCS, Tennessee, lost to Arkansas.

"I don't know how many of you were watching the Arkansas-Tennessee game," I told our team before the game, "but there were a lot of foolish penalties. Don't get caught up in that. Enjoy these times, but concentrate on the next play. When things get big, think small."

It was a very physical game: two teams playing hard for the Big East Championship. And our kids stepped it up. All season, the hotter the situation, the better they liked it. It stemmed from our leaders, Corey Moore and Michael Vick. When your leaders are like that, the rest of the guys will jump in there with them.

We fell behind, 10-0, but never panicked. We kept the pressure on and things began to break. We scored the next 43 points.

We had just posted a huge win against Miami, but in the locker room, Corey Moore was already talking about Temple. Let me tell you, it makes things a whole lot easier when that kind of stuff is coming from within your football team. I think it sinks in with the kids a lot more rather than me having to say it 10 times.

Corey is a really smart guy. He always played with such effort and left everything on the field. I might not always have agreed with everything he said, but he always had the team in mind. He cared so much. He didn't say things just to say them. There was always a reason. And the reason was he really, really cared.

GAME 10
No. 2 Hokies 62, Temple 7
November 20, Philadelphia, Pa.

Before the game I told our kids, "In games like this, when things don't go well, don't panic." We were coming off a couple of very emotional games in a row, and we had a lot at stake. The Owls are a team I always worry about because they can get hot on you. But Michael Vick kind of got hot on them. He had touchdown runs of 53 and 75 yards and threw scoring passes of 65 and 30 yards and we won, 62-7.

The same day, No. 1 Florida State beat No. 3 Florida, which elevated Nebraska to third in the BCS rankings, just 0.63 of a point behind us.

After the game everybody wanted me to talk about Nebraska, but I just wasn't going to do that. It wasn't going to do me any good to talk about "what-ifs" with the media.

It might make good writing, but to me you're talking about something that doesn't need to be talked about. If we deserved to go, we would go. That wasn't a politically correct answer; that was what I really believed in my heart.

GAME 11
No. 2 Hokies 38, No. 22 Boston College 14
November 26, Blacksburg

BC was a pressure game. We not only had to win; we had to win big to keep our standing in the BCS computer polls.

Before the game I told our team, "These are exciting times. This is what we have been talking about all year." Then I repeated the words that had carried us all year. "When things get big, think small. Concentrate on the next play and let's win No. 11."

Our kids played great. We had a season-high 555 yards of total offense. Michael accounted for 366 all by himself — fourth-best in school history. We had six sacks, giving us a Big East single-season record 58.

We won the game, completed our undefeated season and earned our third Big East title.

With about a minute to go, promotions director Tim East came up to me and said he and John Ballein wanted me to say something to the fans after the game. I had no idea what I was going to say. My kickers, Shayne Graham and Jimmy Kibble, carried me out to midfield where Tim had set up a platform. I got up there and it was so crazy, so exciting. I remember everybody in the stadium screaming, and people running out on the field.

I looked down on all these great players and coaches and realized what a fun year it had been. Then I looked around the stands and the field and saw all of those happy Tech fans who had been dreaming of this day for so long. I got filled with so much pride and emotion.

It was a surreal scene. Everybody was celebrating, but they were also watching the scoreboard. Colorado and Nebraska were in overtime. If Colorado won, that was it; we were in the title game. If Nebraska won, there was still a chance they would edge us in the computers. But I didn't think that would happen. I believed what we had done was good enough to get the job done.

"How many of ya'll am I going to see in New Orleans?" I said. It just seemed like the right thing to say. And that roar went up, and it was such a great feeling. Something I wish I could've bottled up and kept forever.

When you can get 54,000 people — fans, students, alumni, professors, townfolk, everybody — all feeling the same way, it is really an amazing thing. And for this one day everybody was united. That was the pinnacle.

Wes Worsham's party for the coaching staff and their immediate family after the game at the Red Lion Inn was like a frat party. Soon, it got out of whack. Everybody crashed it. It was a hand-slapping hugfest. If it was huggable, we hugged it that night.

A few days later, Sports Illustrated came out with Andre Davis on the cover with the headline, "They Belong! Why Virginia Tech Deserves A Shot At The National Title."

"Every time I pick up USA Today or Sports Illustrated, they're writing about us," Cheryl said. "It's almost like they are writing about some other team."

The Sports Illustrated story was great, but as a staff we never really mentioned it. We were focused on things we could control.

On Sunday, December 5th, our team huddled up in the Bowman Club Room of the Jamerson Athletics Center. They were all wearing T-shirts with the number twelve on the front. On the back were the words FINISH IT!

Later that day we got the official word: No. 2 Virginia Tech would play No. 1 Florida State in the 2000 Sugar Bowl for the national championship.

After we got the Sugar Bowl bid, Billy Hite drove down to the grocery store to pick up some milk, bread and eggs. It took him an hour and 15 minutes to get out of the store. There were people coming up to him just wanting to talk. "I could hear someone in the other aisle saying, 'One of the Virginia Tech coaches is in here!' It was a neat feeling," Billy said.

GAME 12
No. 1 Florida State 46, No. 2 Hokies 29
January 4, New Orleans, La.

When we played in the 1995 Sugar Bowl, the New Orleans Riverside Hilton had first choice and took Texas. We stayed at the Le Meridien Hotel, which was great because it was a classy place. But we must have made an impression at that first Sugar Bowl because this time the Hilton picked us. Of course it's a much bigger hotel so there were more fans around.

The Hilton even doubled their security so we could get through all the fans, and the hotel personnel told me they had only done that one other time, when the San Francisco 49ers played in the Super Bowl.

We had a crowd of people lining our path to the bus, everywhere we went.

Corey Moore had his stinger out with the media. He just kind of flipped out on them. I had to sit down and talk to him about it. Even his mother called and told him he was making a fool of himself, and he eased up. I think he was just trying to take the pressure off the other guys.

We decided to have some fun with Corey for our Friday Night Video. We got cornerback Anthony Midget doing some mock interviews with reporters. He looked around and saw tailback Shyrone Stith. "Hey, look, here's Corey Moore," Midget said, pointing at Shyrone. "Why don't you interview him?" The "media" headed toward Shyrone, who started screaming, "Get those cameras out of my face or I'm going to KICK YOUR BUTT!"

That wasn't the only fun thing we did. Earlier in the week, equipment manager Lester Karlin was upset because our practice-shoe order had gotten lost, and he had to give our players these inferior shoes. The players complained about them for a couple of days straight.

One day John Ballein was out jogging by our practice field at Tulane and he saw a big Goodwill dumpster. He got an idea and ran back to our video director, Kevin Hicks. They got Nathaniel Williams in on it.

Now, Nathaniel doesn't say much, but he's a big shoe hound. He always has the latest pair of Nikes. So John got Kevin filming Nathaniel walking down the street with his pair of these awful practice shoes. Nobody watching the video can figure out what's going on. Then Nathaniel stops, makes a face, shakes his head.

And then he throws his pair of shoes into the Goodwill dumpster.

Our players lost it. They started jumping up and down, hooting and hollering. busting on Lester, who was laughing, too.

The night before the game, Bryan Stinespring was doing bed check. Senior centers Keith Short and Tim Schnecker were roommates and liked to have fun with him. Once Short pretended to pass out in the bathtub. Another time he and Schnecker answered the door in nothing but G-strings. They always did something crazy, and Bryan was actually looking forward to seeing what they would come up with for their grand finale.

He went up to their room and knocked. "It's open!" they said.

He walked in, and there the two of them were with a couple of inflatable sheep, ordering them to "baaaa!"

The day of the game, I met with my coaches for our regular gameday meeting at 11 a.m. It was eight hours before the biggest game in Virginia Tech history. I went over special situations, potential fake kicks and so forth. It was really kind of a one-way conversation; Bryan Stinespring looked so nervous he couldn't spit.

I realized I needed to loosen them up. So instead of ending

the meeting with my usual "Go man, go," I said, "You guys coached us into the mess. Now coach us out of it." That broke the tension.

I felt good about our chances to win. Defensively, the question was whether we could get the Seminoles out of their four-wide receiver set. They always start off with that and if they have success, they stay with it. I had also seen some things on film about their alignment that made me feel good about trying a fake. We talked about the fake field goal and the fake punt that morning.

Well, the Seminoles stayed with the four-wide set the whole night. They forced us into having a Whip covering a wideout, and they got a couple of first downs because of that. But where they really got us were the long passes to Peter Warrick. He caught a 64-yarder in the first quarter and a 43-yarder that put the game away in the fourth.

We didn't do a whole lot of things to help our cause. On our first series we drove to the FSU 4-yard line but fumbled. We had a punt blocked for a touchdown, which was set up by a 15-yard intentional grounding call. We had a punt returned for a touchdown, which was set up by a 15-yard offensive pass interference call. And we didn't quite execute a fake field goal and a fake punt.

Both fakes had longer yardage than we wanted them to be. The percentages were against us and Bryan didn't want to try it. I agreed it was a little too long, but I thought we needed to get some things going, make something happen and get things going back our way.

Losing wide receiver Ricky Hall before the game really hurt us. He broke a bone in his foot in practice. We missed having that tall, proven receiver going across the middle. That took away some stuff we wanted to do. Then losing Shyrone hurt. He was really running the ball well, averaging over six yards a carry. Those were two big-time players. Backup tailback Andre

Kendrick stepped in and did a great job, but playing without our No. 1 running back and our No. 2 receiver really made a difference.

We made the great comeback in the third quarter but it wasn't enough. FSU outscored us, 18-0, in the fourth quarter, killing our dreams of a national championship.

In the first chapter I talked about how emotional it was in that locker room. University president Paul Torgersen was in there with us, crying his eyes out.

That loss hurt us bad. I'm not the only one who hasn't watched that tape. Billy Hite told me he can't bear to watch past the third quarter. It was nice that people appreciated our effort and patted our backs, but the fact was we lost the game.

"I'm getting tired of everybody for congratulating us on getting our butts beat," Billy said a few weeks after the game. "Don't get me wrong, I'm proud we played for the national title. But we could have won the thing. That's what makes me want so bad to get back there.

"It makes you hungry."

24

A Lot of People Made It Happen

WHEN I WAS at Radford College getting my master's degree and coaching Radford High School's baseball team, I wanted to win more than anything. I argued with the umpires, argued with the other coach, kicked dirt, made a fool out of myself. I was out of control.

One day basketball coach Carlisle Hostetter came up to me and told me something that has stayed with me to this day.

"When they look back, I really don't think people are going to remember how many baseball games Frank Beamer won at Radford High in 1972," he said. "But I do think they remember how you treated people and what kind of person you were."

I never forgot those words. I'm smart enough to know you've got to win, but I think how you win matters, too.

The formula for being a successful coach is not cut-and-dried. You can't be something you're not. You have to be yourself. I could never be a coach who instilled fear in his players. My approach is different. My deal is that I'm working with you. We're all in this together.

I don't like to brow-beat people. You have to treat people right and treat them with respect. You must have a legitimate interest in them as people. When things get tight at the goal line and you're asking people to lay it out for you, they better feel for you, I'll tell you that. You had better feel for each other. Football is a tough game, but it's not a cold sport. It's all about caring for each other and caring for coaches, and you can't fake that stuff. It has to be there before you're down on that goal line.

I know some coaches want everybody to snap to attention when they walk into a room, but I've never been that way. Many times I'll go into a room and some people won't even know I'm there. Rickey Bustle told me one time I reminded him of Peter Falk's old TV character, "Columbo," except without the ratty raincoat.

And I've seen some guys change when they became a head coach. They thought they had to be something different. I never understood that. You've got to be yourself. I really think I'm the same guy now as I was when we were 2-8-1 in 1992. The only thing different is that more people ask me to speak now.

The key, really, is that the players must respect you. And they won't respect you if you don't know what you're talking about.

I try to be consistent in the way I deal with people, and I want the same from my players. I'd rather have a guy who is consistent over a more talented guy who is up one day and down the next. With those guys, you're going to lose half the time.

I've always believed that good things happen to good

people. If you treat people right and work hard, everything will turn out OK. That's the way I've tried to live my life.

It was nice to be recognized after our undefeated regular season. I won seven Coach of the Year awards: The Associated Press Award, the Paul (Bear) Bryant Award, the Eddie Robinson Award, the Walter Camp Award, the Bobby Dodd Award, the Maxwell Football Club Award and the Football News Coach of the Year Award.

All of these are big time awards — some named after some great people — but the Paul (Bear) Bryant Award was particularly satisfying. If you can win an honor with his name on it, that's special. My ties went back to him through Coach Claiborne. In my mind, Coach Bryant was the guy. If you said the words "college football coach," Bear Bryant would be the guy you were talking about.

On top of that, we had five players selected in the 2000 NFL Draft: John Engelberger and Ike Charlton in round two by San Francisco and Seattle, respectively; Corey Moore in round three, Buffalo; Anthony Midget in round five, Atlanta; and Shyrone Stith, round seven, Jacksonville.

We had eight more guys sign free agent contracts: Placekicker Shayne Graham (Cleveland), punter Jimmy Kibble (New England), defensive tackles Carl Bradley (Tampa Bay) and Nathaniel Williams (Buffalo), wide receiver Ricky Hall (San Francisco), center Keith Short (New York Jets) and linebackers Jamel Smith (New England) and Michael Hawkes (Carolina). This summer we will have an all-time high 13 players in rookie camps.

We are one of only eight teams in the nation to have gone to a bowl the last seven years, and the Big East Conference has allowed us to maximize our potential. With one-third of the country in our viewing area, we are always in the middle of the TV contracts and we have access to big games and the National Championship. But being in the Big East alone didn't do it. We had to have the other basics in place.

1. We have good high school football in Virginia, and we are able to recruit a significant percentage of those players.
2. We have an attractive campus in a beautiful college town.
3. We have a great academic school to sell.
4. We have good facilities that are on the verge of becoming great.
5. We have great fan support. We sold out every home game in 1999 and we always take a lot of people to our bowl games.

We had all those things at Virginia Tech. We were just missing the conference. When we got that avenue, we were able to reach our potential.

I think our setting has a lot of benefits. We're the one school in the Big East that is kinda different.

Blacksburg is in a beautiful part of the country, and there's not much traffic. It's a small college town, so everybody lives about 10 to 15 minutes from campus. That can make a difference if you're staying with a student for some extra work.

In a lot of other places, a 20-minute delay can turn into an hour delay when you start getting into rush hour. Getting home becomes the biggest issue of the day. People start stressing out, getting hurried, and maybe that student doesn't get the care they should get. But when things are more relaxed, people are friendlier and they are more helpful. Our visitors always remark about how friendly we are at Virginia Tech.

When someone says "Virginia Tech," I want people to immediately think "Top Program." Some of that goes beyond winning itself. It's how other people view you: opposing coaching staffs, the media, prospective students.

Do you do things the right way? Do you run a good program? Do you win your share of the ballgames? Some years you're going to do better than others, but at least I always want to be knocking on the door for the Big East Championship. We always want to be a dangerous team, in the mix every year.

That's beginning to happen now. We've come such a long way from those early years, when every game was a struggle. There were some changes made but we kept fighting. And we did something very few schools ever do.

We were able to change the status of our program.

Virginia Tech is now perceived in a totally different light. I can see it in the way our fans react to us, in the way the ESPN people treat us, how *Sports Illustrated* approaches us. How other coaches act toward us.

When I sit here and think how the stadium is going to look in 2001 and 2002, I get very excited. Some schools might have a place that seats more, but our place is going to be great. Those stands go straight up and our fans are right on top of the action. There are no bad seats.

To me the future is bright. I think the best days are still ahead. Playing for the national championship was great, but that is not going to be the last time we do it. We're going to be back. I say that knowing how hard it was to get to get there the first time.

I'm happy with our success, but it bothers me that four family members were not alive to see that 1999 season. My dad, Cheryl's father, Mr. Oakley; Waddey Harvey and Uncle Rufus Beamer, who was one of my father's three brothers. He was former head of the vocation educational department at Virginia Tech. Those people meant so much to me and were such big fans. They really would have enjoyed our 1999 season.

They were with us for all those tough early years, when playing for the national championship would have seemed laughable.

Who knows; maybe they're watching after all.

This spring (2000) it seemed like it rained every day. We

scheduled a scrimmage for one Saturday but it was rained out. We rescheduled it for Monday. My secretary, Diana Clark, checked the weather reports for me and we concluded that it was going to rain around 4 p.m. So we canceled our early meetings and moved the scrimmage up from 4:25 to 3:30 p.m.

It was raining as the team went through the tunnel to Lane Stadium, but when we emerged, it stopped. We were hoping to get two quarters in, but the rain held off for two hours and we completed the full four-quarter scrimmage.

As we walked off the field, on cue, it began to pour again. People used to say Coach Bryant could order the weather, and that day I guess I felt a little like him. It's probably as close as I will ever get to that feeling, I suppose, but I think I had a little help that day.

Maybe, just maybe, dad, Mr. Oakley, Uncle Rufus and Waddey had something to do with it.

THE BEAMER RECORD

Year	School	Record
1981	Murray State	8-3-0
1982	Murray State	4-7-0
1983	Murray State	7-4-0
1984	Murray State	9-2-0
1985	Murray State	7-3-1
1986	Murray State	7-4-1*
1987	Virginia Tech	2-9-0
1988	Virginia Tech	3-8-0
1989	Virginia Tech	6-4-1
1990	Virginia Tech	6-5-0
1991	Virginia Tech	5-6-0
1992	Virginia Tech	2-8-1
1993	Virginia Tech	9-3-0
1994	Virginia Tech	8-4-0
1995	Virginia Tech	10-2-0**
1996	Virginia Tech	10-2-0***
1997	Virginia Tech	7-5-0
1998	Virginia Tech	9-3-0
1999	Virginia Tech	11-1-0**
TOTAL		130-83-4

* Ohio Valley co-champion
** Big East champion
*** Big East co-champion

ABOUT THE
AUTHORS

FRANK BEAMER is the head football coach at Virginia Tech. Since taking over at his alma mater, he has posted a record of 88-60-2, won 3 Big East titles and led the Hokies to seven straight bowl games. After the 1999 season, he was voted every major Coach of the Year award. He previously coached at Murray State (Ky.), where he led the Racers to a record of 42-23-2 in six seasons and an Ohio Valley co-championship in 1986.

CHRIS COLSTON is a sports features writer with *Baseball Weekly*. He previously was the editor of Virginia Tech's *Hokie Huddler*, the official magazine covering Virginia Tech athletics. Colston has also authored the books, *Rare Birds: A Look at the Baltimore Orioles* and *Hokies Handbook: Stories, Stats & Stuff About Virginia Tech Football*.